# HAL LEONARD KEYBOARD STYLE SERIES

# MODERN POP KEYBOARD

## THE COMPLETE GUIDE WITH AUDIO!

### BY MARK HARRISON

**PLAYBACK+**
Speed • Pitch • Balance • Loop

To access audio, visit:
**www.halleonard.com/mylibrary**

8569-1867-2629-4276

ISBN 978-1-4950-2507-5

Visit Hal Leonard Online at **www.halleonard.com**

Explore the entire family of Hal Leonard products and resources

 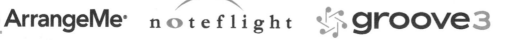 

World headquarters, contact:
**Hal Leonard**
7777 West Bluemound Road
Milwaukee, WI 53213
Email: info@halleonard.com

In Europe, contact:
**Hal Leonard Europe Limited**
1 Red Place
London, W1K 6PL
Email: info@halleonardeurope.com

In Australia, contact:
**Hal Leonard Australia Pty. Ltd.**
4 Lentara Court
Cheltenham, Victoria, 3192 Australia
Email: info@halleonard.com.au

# INTRODUCTION

**W**elcome to *Modern Pop Keyboard*. If you're interested in playing today's contemporary pop styles on the piano and synthesizer, but are not quite sure how, then you've come to the right place! Whatever your playing level, this book will help you sound more authentic in your modern pop stylings.

After reviewing some essential chords and scales, we'll dig into the voicing techniques and patterns that are vital for the contemporary pop keyboard player. As well as focusing on chordal "comping" (or accompaniment), we'll also develop important single-line techniques such as arpeggios and ostinatos. All this will help you create your own keyboard parts on a variety of modern pop songs and progressions.

Today's keyboard arrangements are different from the "classic" keyboard parts we associate with 20th-century pop music. Nowadays a minimal approach (playing partial chords or single-note lines) is often needed from the keyboard player, giving more space and a lighter touch to the arrangement. Also, as 21st-century pop styles have evolved, traditional notions about keyboard textures and orchestration have given way to edgier, more experimental sounds and combinations.

Five complete songs in various modern pop styles are included in the "Style File" chapter at the end of the book. Jam with the rhythm section on these tunes using the online audio. This is a great way to develop your keyboard chops within these different rhythmic styles. Good luck with your Modern Pop Keyboard!

*–Mark Harrison*

## About the Online Audio

The online audio features demonstrations of most of the music examples in the book. The solo keyboard tracks feature the left-hand part on the left channel, and the right-hand part on the right channel, for easy "hands separate" practice. The full band tracks feature the rhythm section on the left channel and the keyboard on the right channel, so that you can play along with the band. This is all designed to give you maximum flexibility when practicing! Please see the individual chapters for specific information on the audio tracks and how to use them.

## About the Author

Mark Harrison is a professional keyboardist, composer/arranger, and music educator/author based in Los Angeles. He has worked with top musicians such as Jay Graydon (Steely Dan), John Molo (Bruce Hornsby band), Jimmy Haslip (Yellowjackets), and numerous others. Mark has recorded three CDs with his contemporary jazz band (the Mark Harrison Quintet), and plays regularly on the Los Angeles club and festival circuit with the Steely Dan tribute band Doctor Wu. His TV music credits include *Saturday Night Live*, *The Montel Williams Show*, *American Justice*, *Celebrity Profiles*, *America's Most Wanted*, *True Hollywood Stories*, and many others.

Mark has also become one of the most in-demand contemporary music educators in Los Angeles. He taught at the renowned Grove School of Music for six years, instructing hundreds of musicians from all around the world. Mark was also invited to join the University of Southern California's Popular Music faculty during the 2013-14 school year, working alongside world-famous musicians such as Patrice Rushen, Ndugu Chancler, and Alfonso Johnson.

Mark currently runs a busy private teaching studio, catering to the needs of professional and aspiring musicians alike. His students include Grammy-winners, hit songwriters, members of the Boston Pops and L.A. Philharmonic orchestras, and first-call touring musicians with major acts. Mark's music instruction books are used by thousands of musicians in over 20 countries, and are recommended by the Berklee College of Music for all their new students. He has also written Master Class articles for *Keyboard* and *How to Jam* magazines, covering a variety of keyboard styles and topics. For further information on Mark's musical activities, education products, and online lessons, please visit *www.harrisonmusic.com*.

# CONTENTS

# Chapter 1

# WHAT IS MODERN POP?

For the purposes of this book, we're using "modern pop" as a catch-all term encompassing popular music styles of the 21st century so far. Over the last few decades, the role of piano and keyboards in pop styles has been rather cyclical in nature. For example, the synth-heavy pop sounds of the 1980s gave way to the guitar-driven pop/rock sounds of the 1990s. Fast forward to the latter half of the 2010s, and we now see piano and synthesizers being used in ever more interesting ways, providing essential rhythmic and harmonic definition, as well as an ever-expanding palette of tonal colors.

In the 2010s, we also witness an emphasis on simplicity in the keyboard parts for most pop songs. Piano and synth lines are often sparse and uncluttered in nature, with chordal parts using more "open" and less dense voicings. This is in specific contrast to the keyboard approach taken in some of the pop styles of the last millenium. We'll get into these "modern" approaches to keyboard parts later in this book.

Generally, there have been significant industry trends that influence pop music styles in the 21st century. Declining CD sales, together with illegal music downloading over the Internet, impacted record company budgets and arguably led to more formula-based and less creative commercial releases during the 2000s. By the 2010s however, paid download portals such as iTunes had gone some way toward restoring pop music sales revenue. Other significant trends affecting pop music in this millennium are song placements in movies and TV shows (almost today's equivalent of getting a record deal back in the 20th century), pop careers originating from singers on TV talent shows, and the extensive influence of electronic dance music across the spectrum of today's pop styles.

Democratization of the recording and production process is another huge factor affecting pop music in this millennium. Most commercial pop songs and albums in the 20th century were recorded in larger professional studios, at significant cost. By contrast, today's faster computers and lower-cost music and recording equipment have empowered legions of home and project studios, enabling talented musicians to produce music with a quality rivaling the top commercial facilities. This is related to the rise and influence of electronic dance music (EDM) as mentioned above, in that EDM genres are particularly suitable for today's ubiquitous computer-based music production.

Next we'll explore in detail how to build your own modern pop keyboard parts, starting with some essential scales and chords in Chapter 2. On with the show!

# Chapter 2
# SCALES AND CHORDS

## Major Scales

First, let's take a look at the major scale, the fundamental basis of harmony in most contemporary music styles, including modern pop. Think of this scale in terms of the intervals it contains (i.e., whole step, whole step, half step, whole step, whole step, whole step, half step), as this most closely parallels how the ear relates to the scale. Here is the C major scale, showing these intervals:

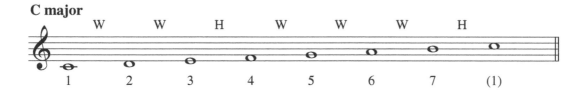

For your reference, here are all the major scales. After the first scale (C major), the next seven scales contain flats; i.e., F major has one flat, B♭ major has two flats, and so on. The next seven scales contain sharps; i.e., G major has one sharp, D major has two sharps, and so on.

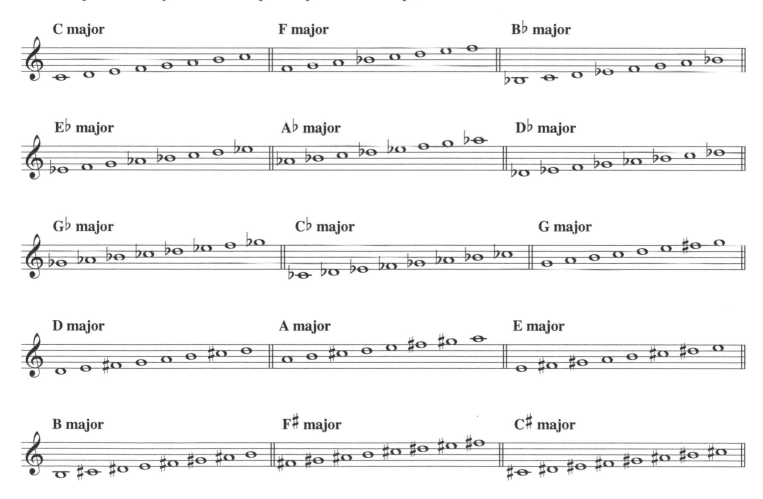

In this book, we'll work with music examples in different major and minor keys. For example, a tune will be "in the key of C major" if the note C is heard as the tonic or "home base," and if the notes used are within the C major scale, except for any sharped or flatted notes occurring in the music. Similarly, a tune will be "in the key of A minor" if the note A is heard as the tonic or "home base," and if the notes used are within the A natural minor scale (again, except for any sharped or flatted notes).

A key signature is a group of flats or sharps at the beginning of the music that lets you know which key you are in. Each key signature works for both a major and a minor key, which are considered relative to one another. For example, the first key signature shown below (no sharps and no flats) works for the keys of both C major and A minor. To find out which minor key shares the same key signature as a major key, we can take the 6th degree of the corresponding major scale; i.e., the 6th degree of a C major scale is the note A, so the keys of C major and A minor are relative to one another and share the same key signature.

For your reference, here are all the major and minor key signatures:

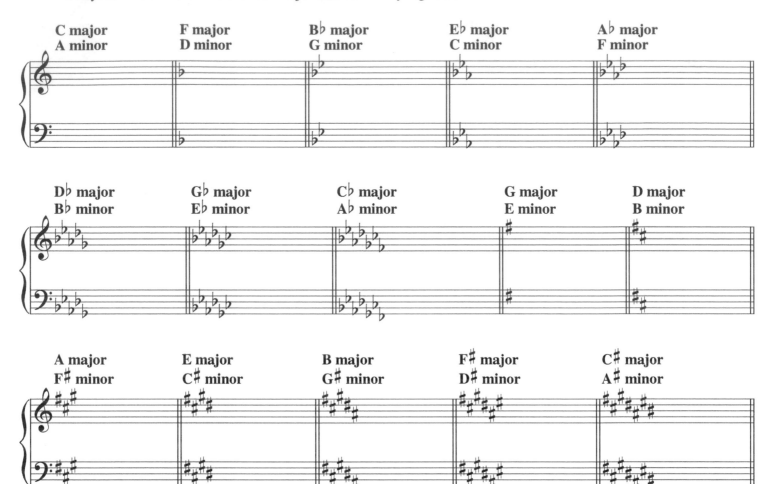

# Pentatonic Scales

The pentatonic scale (a.k.a. the major pentatonic scale) is a five-note scale often used in modern pop styles. It can be derived by taking the major scale and removing the 4th and 7th degrees:

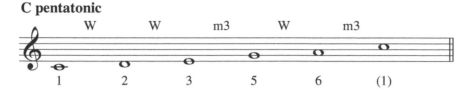

Note that, from bottom to top, this scale contains the following intervals: whole step, whole step, minor 3rd, whole step, and minor 3rd.

The minor pentatonic scale (a.k.a. blues pentatonic) can be derived from the above pentatonic scale. For example, if we now take the C pentatonic scale and displace it to start on the note A (the relative minor of C), we create an A minor pentatonic scale:

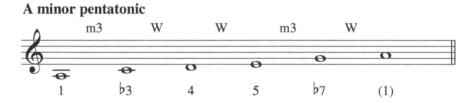

From bottom to top, this scale now contains the following intervals: minor 3rd, whole step, whole step, minor 3rd, and whole step.

# Natural Minor Scales

Next we'll take a look at the most frequently used minor scale in contemporary pop: the natural minor scale. If we stay within a minor key without using any extra accidentals (sharps or flats) in the music, that means we are working within a natural minor scale restriction. Again, it is good to think of this scale in terms of the intervals it contains. Here is the A natural minor scale, showing these intervals:

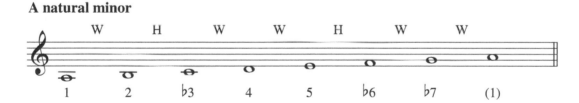

# Triads and Suspensions

There are four main types of triads (three-part chords) in common usage: major, minor, augmented, and diminished. (Of these, the major and minor triads are by far the most pervasive in modern pop styles). The following example shows all four of these triads, built from the root of C in each case:

These triads are formed by building the following intervals above the root note:

Major triad:           Major 3rd and perfect 5th (1–3–5)

Minor triad:           Minor 3rd and perfect 5th (1–♭3–5)

Augmented triad:   Major 3rd and augmented 5th (1–3–♯5)

Diminished triad:   Minor 3rd and diminished 5th (1–♭3–♭5)

A suspension of a major or minor triad occurs when the 3rd of the chord is replaced with another chord tone, most commonly the 4th (also referred to as the 11th). The 9th (also referred to as the 2nd) can also be added to a major or minor triad, either instead of or in addition to the 3rd:

Note the alternate chord symbols above the staff, which you may encounter for these chords:

- In measure 1, we have replaced the 3rd of a major or minor triad with the 4th/11th. If "sus" is used without a number following it in the chord symbol, the 4th/11th is assumed.

- In measure 2, we have replaced the 3rd of a major or minor triad with the 9th/2nd.

- In measure 3, we have added the 9th/2nd to a major triad.

- In measure 4, we have added the 9th/2nd to a minor triad.

All these are signature sounds in modern pop keyboard styles, as we will see in later examples.

## Diatonic Triads in Major and Minor

If we construct triads from each degree of the major scale, and stay within the restrictions of the scale, we create diatonic triads within that major key. The following example shows the diatonic triads found within the C major scale:

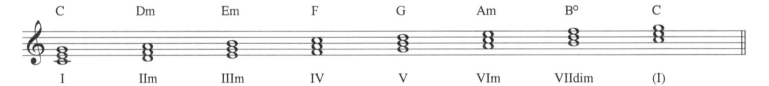

Relating the above triads to the four main triad types we saw earlier, note that major triads are built from the 1st, 4th, and 5th major scale degrees, minor triads are built from the 2nd, 3rd, and 6th scale degrees, and a diminished triad is built from the 7th scale degree. (The augmented triad does not occur anywhere in the diatonic series.)

For modern pop songs in major keys, we primarily use the I, IV, and V major triads, and the II, III, and VI minor triads. These six chords have been the basis of innumerable hit songs for decades, and show no signs of going out of fashion in 21st-century pop styles!

Moving on to the natural minor scale we saw earlier: if we construct triads from each degree of this scale, and stay within the restrictions of the scale, we create diatonic triads within that minor key. The following example shows the diatonic triads found within the A natural minor scale:

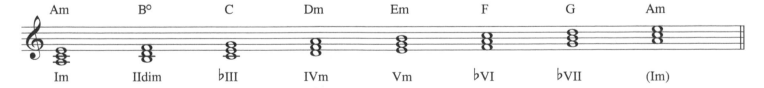

Again relating the above triads to the four main triad types we saw earlier, note that minor triads are now built from the 1st, 4th, and 5th major scale degrees, major triads are built from the ♭3rd, ♭6th, and ♭7th scale degrees, and a diminished triad is built from the 2nd scale degree.

For modern pop songs in minor keys, we primarily use the I, IV, and V minor triads, and the ♭III, ♭VI, and ♭VII major triads.

# Seventh (or Four-Part) Chords

Although the majority of modern pop harmony is triad-based, there will be times (particularly with R&B-influenced pop styles) where four-part chords will be needed. The term "seventh chord" is sometimes used to describe four-part chords in which the highest note or extension is the 7th. The four-part chords most ordinarily used in contemporary styles are the major 7th, major 6th, minor 7th, minor 6th, dominant 7th, and suspended dominant 7th chords. The following example shows these four-part chords, built from the root of C:

These chords are formed by building the following intervals above the root note:

Major 7th chord:      major 3rd, perfect 5th, and major 7th intervals

Major 6th chord:      major 3rd, perfect 5th, and major 6th intervals

Minor 7th chord:      minor 3rd, perfect 5th, and minor 7th intervals

Minor 6th chord:      minor 3rd, perfect 5th, and major 6th intervals

Dominant 7th chord: major 3rd, perfect 5th, and minor 7th intervals

Suspended Dominant 7th chord:
                     perfect 4th, perfect 5th, and minor 7th intervals.

In this chapter, we've summarized the essential music theory and harmony that will help you play modern pop keyboard styles. If you would like further information on these topics, please check out my other music instruction books, *Contemporary Music Theory* (Levels 1–3) and *The Pop Piano Book*. (All of these books are published by Hal Leonard Corporation.)

# Chapter 3

# HARMONY AND VOICINGS

## Voicing Concepts

Let's start out by defining what is meant by "voicing," for the modern pop keyboard player. A voicing is a specific allocation of notes on the keyboard, chosen to interpret a chord symbol in a stylistic way. For example, in Chapter 2 (page 7) we saw how to spell a C major triad (containing the notes C, E, and G). If we needed to play a C major chord during a song, we might indeed choose to play it exactly in this manner. However, there are other ways we might choose to interpret (or "voice") this C major chord:

- We could play the triad in a different "inversion," meaning a different sequence of notes from bottom to top. This is particularly useful when we want to connect smoothly from one chord to the next, which most contemporary styles, including modern pop, require us to do.

- We could play "dyads," sounding two notes instead of three. This lighter, more open sound is routinely heard in 21st century pop songs, as we will see in later examples. (See page 14.)

- We could play "open" triads, re-distributing the notes to cover a range greater than one octave. This broad, powerful sound is useful for synth parts as well as piano.

- We could play the the triad in "arpeggiated" (broken-chord) style, articulating one note at a time to create a rhythmic pattern or texture.

In this chapter we will develop these and other ways to voice chords, all of which will be useful for the modern pop keyboardist.

The online audio tracks for this chapter all have the left-hand part on the left channel, the right-hand part on the right channel, and a hi-hat click in the middle. The tracks are recorded using a grand piano sound, except where noted in the text.

## Major and Minor Triad Inversions

As mentioned above, inversions of triads are used regularly in contemporary styles. Here are the inversions of a C major triad:

Note that, in the above example, the first triad shown is in root position (with the root on the bottom), the second triad is in first inversion (with the root on top), and the third triad is in second inversion (with the root in the middle). The last triad is in root position, an octave higher than the first. To connect smoothly between successive voicings, it is important to have these inversions under your fingers in all keys. You should make it a goal to learn all the major triad inversions:

TRACK 1

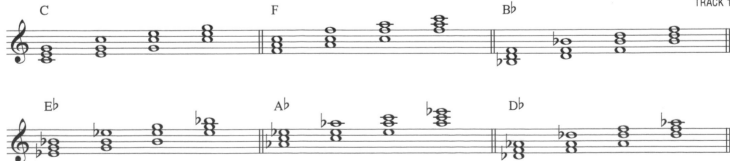

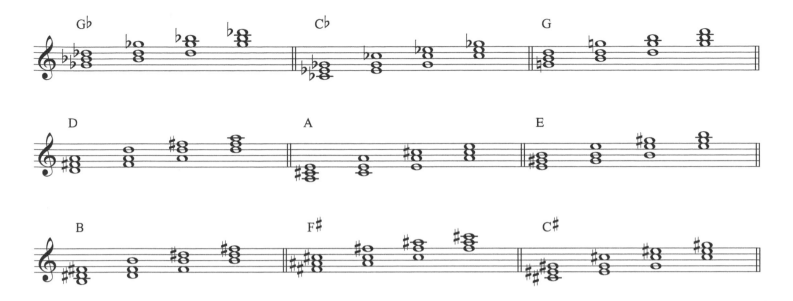

Next up, we have the inversions of a C minor triad:

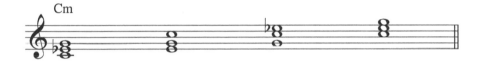

The above example contains C minor triads in root position, first inversion, second inversion, and then root position again, similar to the previous major triad examples.

You should learn these inversions in all keys, as shown in the following example:

TRACK 2

Now it's time to look at the keyboard part for a chord progression, using some of the techniques covered so far:

- **Diatonic triads.** In Chapter 2 (page 8) we saw the diatonic triads in the key of C major. The following progression will be chosen from these chords.

- **Triad inversions.** Rather than using root-position triads, as first seen in Chapter 2, we will instead use inversions as shown for the preceding audio Tracks 1 and 2. This will yield a more connected, musical result.

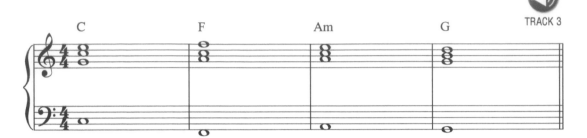

In the above example, note that:

- In the right hand, the C major triad is in second inversion, the F major triad is in first inversion, and the A minor and G major triads are in root position. There are various other triad inversions that could have been used, and you are of course encouraged to experiment with this.

- In the left hand, the root of each chord is being played. This is a common technique in the simpler pop styles.

# Triad Arpeggios

Next we will apply right-hand triad arpeggios to the same chord progression. An arpeggio simply means playing the notes of the chord one at a time, or broken-chord style. In this example, the arpeggio employs eighth notes (which last for half-a-beat each). Arpeggios are an enduringly popular device across the range of contemporary styles, and are used pervasively in modern pop songs.

The arpeggios are based on the same triad inversions as used for audio Track 3. On the piano recording, the sustain pedal is used to blend the notes together within each chord. When playing this example, be sure to release the sustain pedal at the point of chord change, so that you don't inadvertently mix chord tones together between adjacent chords.

# Triads Placed Over 3rd or 5th in Bass

In the preceding example, the keyboard left-hand part is playing the root of each chord (C below the C major chord, F below the F major chord, etc.). Although this is very common, sometimes we'll need to place a note other than the root of the chord in the bass, or lowest voice. For modern pop, the most conventional options will be to play either the 3rd or the 5th in the bass, as shown in the following chord progression in the key of A minor:

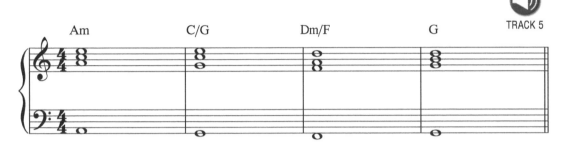

In this progression, the C major triad has been placed over its 5th in the bass, and the D minor triad has been placed over its 3rd in the bass. Note the chord symbols shown in the second and third measures: C/G means "C major triad placed over G in the bass," and Dm/F means "D minor triad placed over F in the bass."

This technique creates an interesting and useful musical effect. The vertical quality of the C major and D minor chords has changed with the new bass notes, and the left-hand line has a smooth, melodic character.

When we place different notes in the bass like this, it is called "inverting" the chord, as in a "C major chord inverted over its 5th (G)." This is a correct description; however, note that the term "inversion" is used a little differently, compared to the triad inversions at the start of this chapter (where we were simply re-ordering the notes of triad from top to bottom, with no bass note implications). The term "inversion" can therefore be used within these different musical contexts.

Also note that all the triads used in this example are diatonic to the key of A minor. See Chapter 2 (page 8) for the diatonic triads available within the A natural minor scale.

# Alternating-Eighths Patterns

Next we will take the chord progression from the preceding example and apply a right-hand alternating-eighths pattern to it. This involves splitting the right-hand triads so that the upper notes land on all the beats (beats 1, 2, 3, and 4, in a measure of 4/4 time), and the lower note is then played a half a beat (one eighth note) later:

Compare this example to Track 5. You'll see that the right-hand triads and inversions are same; they've simply been split to creating the alternating pattern described above. This keyboard device is used every day in classic as well as modern pop styles.

# Dyads and Open-Triad Voicings

Next we will explore further useful ways to voice triads. These are advantageous for the modern pop keyboardist.

Instead of playing all three notes of a major or minor triad, we might choose to play only two, resulting in what some textbooks and methods call a "dyad." This will effect a lighter, less-dense texture; it is well-known in 21st-century pop styles. Let's see this technique at work, using a diatonic triad progression in the key of E♭ major:

TRACK 7

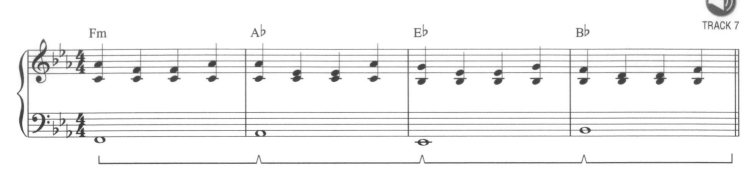

Listen to the audio track to hear this lighter, more open texture compared to full triads. For example, the first measure is based on a second-inversion F minor triad (see Track 2, second measure, third chord), the second measure is based on a first-inversion A♭ major triad (see Track 1, fifth measure, second chord), and so on.

In this example, each dyad lasts for one beat, creating a steady, rhythmically consistent pattern. Other rhythms can also be applied to the same voicings, as in the following:

TRACK 8

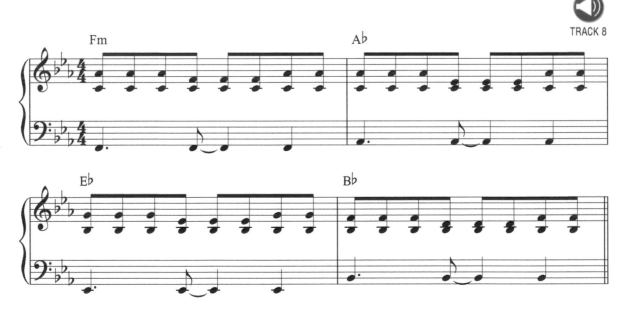

This example uses the same dyad voicings as Track 7, but now with a steady eighth-note rhythm in the right hand, together with rhythmic syncopations in the left hand. (In Chapter 4, there's much more to come about eighth-note rhythms, counting, and syncopations.)

Next we'll look the "open-triad" voicing technique. An open triad occurs when we redistribute the notes of the triad to cover a range greater than one octave. This most often happens when we take the middle note of a triad and move it up by an octave, as in the following example in the key of C minor:

TRACK 9

Note the broad, powerful sound created when the triad voicings are opened up in this manner. This example uses various eighth-note rhythms and syncopations. (There's more about this in Chapter 4.)

Comparing the first C minor voicing above to the C minor triad shown at the beginning of Track 2, we see that instead of the basic C minor chord stack of C–E♭–G, we instead have C–G–E♭ from bottom to top, with the overall span being greater than one octave.

These open triads can also be used in arpeggio (broken-chord) form. This is a traditional left-hand technique in pop ballad styles, as in the following example:

TRACK 10

The left-hand patterns here use the same notes as in Track 9, now placed in the left hand and using a repeated eighth-eighth-quarter note rhythm. Note also the dyad voicings in the right-hand part. This is all typical of modern pop ballad styles.

The next two examples are recorded using a fat, analog synth sound characteristic of today's pop and EDM styles.

# Ostinato Lines

The use of keyboard ostinatos has become a signature sound in 21st-century pop music. An ostinato is the name given to a musical line that is repeated across different chord changes. In the following A major example, the right hand is playing a repeated E–A–G♯–A eighth-note line over a diatonic chord progression:

TRACK 11

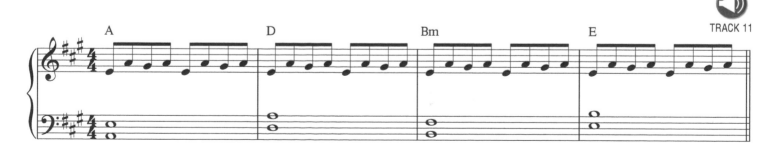

Here, the left hand is playing simple root-5th voicings, anchoring each chord below the ostinato line. In comparison to the triad voicing examples we've seen earlier, this can sound more interesting and sophisticated. This is, in part, because the ostinato line is adding upper extensions/alterations to the chords. For example:

- Over the A major chord in the first measure, the G# is the 7th of the chord.
- Over the D major chord in the second measure, the E and G# are the 9th and sharped 11th of the chord, respectively.
- And so on.

The bottom line: You are likely to get away with adding these extensions onto the chords, provided: 1) the ostinato line has a nice melodic "hook" to it; 2) both the ostinato and the underlying chord progression belong to the same major or minor key. (Most of the time, pop musicians work this out by ear, but knowing these harmonic principles can help give you a head start in this area.)

Ostinato lines do not have to be rhythmically consistent, as in the preceding example. They may use more rhythmic variation and syncopations:

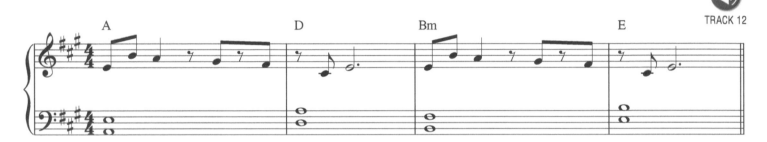

Again, upper extensions and out-of-chord tones occur here. The ear will generally forgive these due to melodic and rhythmic nature of the ostinato line over the changes.

Although a great deal of modern pop songs use basic triad harmony, there may be times when you'll want more sophisticated sounds in your bag of tricks. To that end, we'll take a deep breath and look at some more advanced voicing techniques.

# Upper Structure Triad Voicings

To voice larger (i.e., four-part) chords, place a triad in the right hand over the root of the chord in the left hand. The right-hand triad will then be an "upper structure" of the overall chord. We see this voicing approach in the following example, recorded with a grand piano sound:

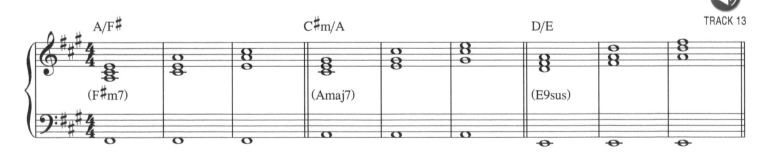

Looking at the first measure in this example, we see a voicing for an F# minor 7th chord.

Instead of playing all the notes of this chord (F#–A–C–E) in the right hand, we have instead split off the upper three notes (A–C#–E, equivalent to an A major triad) for the right-hand part, leaving the root (F#) in the lower register in the left hand. The next two measures show different inversions of the upper A major triad, again placed over F# in the left hand. We could say that we are "building a major triad from the 3rd of the minor 7th chord" in the right hand, as the note A (the root of the right-hand major triad) is the third of the overall F# minor 7th chord. This is a familiar and highly effective voicing for a minor 7th chord, across a range of pop music styles.

Similarly, in the second measure of this example, we see a voicing for an Amaj7 chord. Instead of playing all the notes of this chord (A–C#–E–G#) in the right hand, we have instead split off the upper three notes (C#–E–G#, equivalent to a C# minor triad) for the right-hand part, leaving the root (A) in the lower register in the left hand. The next two measures show different inversions of the upper C# minor triad, again placed over A in the left hand. We could say that we are "building a minor triad from the 3rd of the major 7th chord" in the right hand, as the note C# (the root of the right-hand minor triad) is the 3rd of the overall Amaj7 chord. Again, this is a useful voicing for major 7th chords in pop styles.

In the last three measures of this example, we see that a D major triad has been "built from" the 7th of an E9sus chord (the suspended dominant 9th is a larger version of the suspended dominant 7th chord we saw on page 9 in Chapter 2). Technically, this gives us the 7th, 9th, and 11th (4th) of the overall chord, and is probably the most oft-repeated keyboard voicing for "suspended dominant" chords in pop music styles.

A final note on the chord symbols in the preceding example: The symbols shown between the staffs (F#m7, Amaj7, etc) are **composite** chord symbols you are more likely to see on actual charts. The symbols shown above the treble staff (A/F#, C#m/A, etc.) are the slash chord symbol equivalents, shown here to illustrate the upper structure triad voicing concepts. These are also perfectly valid chord symbols, but you are more likely to see their composite symbol counterparts on charts.

## Static and Rhythmic Chordal Pads

Now let's use these new upper structure triad voicings in a chord progression in the key of F# minor. This will help us demonstrate the idea of using "chordal pads" in modern pop keyboard parts. The term "pad" is often associated with a static, mellow-sounding synthesizer layer added to an arrangement. Technically though, a pad can be any use of a chordal sound in an arrangement, whether static or in a rhythmic pattern.

The next two audio examples are recorded using a bright, sawtooth/square wave layered synth with "oscillator sync," resulting in a biting sound with rich tone colors.

First up is a "static pad" keyboard part using the preceding upper structure triad voicings:

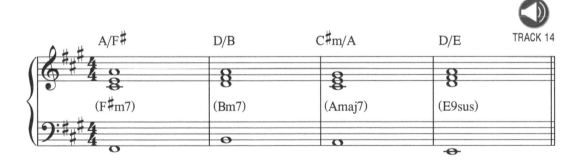

Here's a quick review of the voicings used in this example:

- In measure 1, the F#m7 is voiced by building an A major triad from the 3rd (see Track 13, second measure).

- In measure 2, the Bm7 is voiced by building a D major triad from the 3rd (same technique as for the F#m7 chord, now applied to Bm7).

- In measure 3, the Amaj7 is voiced by building a C# minor triad from the 3rd (see Track 13, fourth measure).

- In measure 4, the E9sus is voiced by building a D major triad from the 7th (see Track 13, seventh measure).

Next we have a "rhythmic pad" example using the same voicings:

TRACK 15

This example now uses 16th-note rhythms and syncopations, suitable for various R&B/pop keyboard styles. (There's more about 16th-note rhythms and counting in Chapter 4.)

# Double-4th Voicings

In this section we'll look at one more advanced keyboard voicing technique using "double 4ths." In my books and classes, I define a double-4th as a shape consisting of two consecutive perfect 4th intervals. For example, if we start with the note E♭ and add the note a perfect 4th above, that would be A♭. If we then add another note a perfect fourth above the A♭, we get to D♭. This in total gives us the three-note shape B♭–E♭–A♭. This hip, transparent configuration originates from jazz styles, but can be the pop keyboardist's secret weapon as a more stylish alternative to triad voicings. Here are a couple more important things you should know about double-4ths:

- They can be inverted (root position, first inversion, second inversion) in a similar way to triads.

- They can be placed over different notes in the bass, to create/imply various chord qualities, in a manner similar to the upper structure triads seen earlier.

With these points in mind, we'll look at the next example (recorded with an acoustic piano sound), which takes the above-mentioned E♭–A♭–D♭ double-4th, inverts it, and places it over various roots in the key of D♭ major:

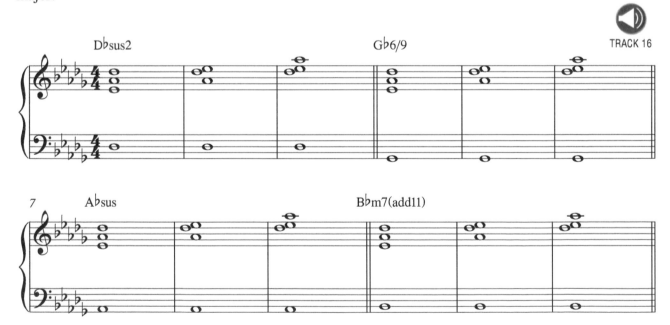

TRACK 16

In each group of three measures in this example, the right hand is playing the E♭–A♭–D♭ double-4th: first in root position, then in first inversion, then in second inversion.

Let's explore the voicings used in this example:

- In Measures 1–3, the E♭–A♭–D♭ double-4th is placed over D♭ in the bass. We could say that the double-4th has been "built from the 9th of the chord" as E♭ is the 9th of a D♭ major chord. This technically creates the D♭sus2 as shown; however, you could apply this to a simple D♭ major chord symbol if you wanted to upgrade your voicing with this stylish sound.

- In Measures 4–6, the E♭–A♭–D♭ double-4th is placed over G♭ in the bass. We could say that the double-4th has been "built from the 6th of the chord" as E♭ is the 6th of a G♭ major chord. This technically creates the G♭6/9 as shown; however, you could apply this to a simple G♭ major chord symbol if desired. (Use with caution, as this has a jazzier sound.)

- In Measures 7–9, the E♭–A♭–D♭ double-4th is placed over A♭ in the bass. We could say that the double-4th has been "built from the 5th of the chord," as E♭ is the 5th of the A♭ suspended (or sus4) chord.

- In Measures 10–12, the E♭–A♭–D♭ double-4th is placed over B♭ in the bass. We could say that the double-4th has been "built from the 11th of the chord," as E♭ is the 11th (or 4th) of a B♭ minor chord. This technically creates the B♭m7(add11) shown; however, you could apply this to a simple B♭ minor chord symbol if desired.

For a cool example of using these various upper structure double-4th voicings, and in the key of D♭ as shown here, check out the great Maroon5 song "My Heart Is Open."

The next two audio examples are recorded using a synth/clav layered sound, with a short attack and full sustain. First up is a "static pad" keyboard part using the preceding upper structure double-4th voicings, over a diatonic progression in the key of D♭:

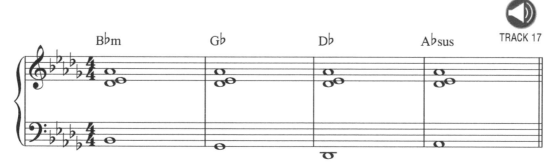

Note that the upper structure double-4th E♭–A♭–D♭ is used in second inversion throughout. Also, these right-hand voicings are shown an octave lower compared to those on Track 16. Here's a quick review of the voicings used in this cxample:

- In measure 1, the B♭ minor chord is voiced by building the E♭–A♭–D♭ double-4th from the 4th/11th. (See Track 16, twelfth measure.)

- In measure 2, the G♭ major chord is voiced by building the E♭–A♭–D♭ double-4th from the 6th. (See Track 16, sixth measure.)

- In measure 3, the D♭ major chord is voiced by building the E♭–A♭–D♭ double-4th from the 9th. (See Track 16, third measure.)

- In measure 4, the A♭ suspended (or sus4) chord is voiced by building the E♭–A♭–D♭ double-4th from the 5th. (See Track 16, ninth measure.)

Next we have a "rhythmic pad" example using the same voicings:

This example uses 16th-note rhythmic figures, suitable for pop/funk and dance styles.

In Chapter 4, we'll get to use these voicing tools within various rhythmic and stylistic contexts, to create an assortment of modern pop keyboard parts for both piano and synthesizers!

# Chapter 4
# STYLES

Now we'll apply the keyboard harmony covered in Chapter 3 to create authentic keyboard patterns in a variety of modern pop styles. First, let's review the rhythmic subdivisions used in contemporary pop music.

## Rhythmic Concepts

Most modern pop styles are written in 4/4 time and use patterns based around eighth or 16th notes. Each of these subdivisions can be played straight or swing, essentially resulting in four main rhythmic styles or groups:

- Straight eighths

- Swing eighths

- Straight 16ths

- Swing 16ths

In a straight-eighths feel, each eighth note is of equal length and divides the beat exactly in half:

TRACK 19

Note the rhythmic counting above the staff. This is how eighth-note rhythms are normally counted, with the 1, 2, 3, and 4 falling on the **downbeats**, and the "&s" falling halfway in between, on the **upbeats**.

In a swing-eighths feel, the second eighth note in each beat (the "&" in the rhythmic counting) lands two-thirds of the way through the beat. This is equivalent to playing on the first and third parts of an eighth-note triplet. We still count using "1 & 2 &," etc., but now each "&" is played a little later:

TRACK 20

The first measure above looks the same as the previous straight-eighths example, but when a swing eighths interpretation is applied to it, it sounds equivalent to the second measure above (i.e., the quarter-eighth triplets). However, as the second measure above is more cumbersome to write and to read, it is standard practice to notate as in the first measure above, but to interpret in a swing-eighths rhythmic style as needed.

There will also be times when we need to access the middle note (i.e., the second part) of an eighth-note triplet, within an overall swing-eighths feel. In this case, we would notate using a triplet sign; however, all the other eighth-note pairs (without triplet signs) would still be interpreted as swing eighths. If a tune needed a lot of triplet signs for this reason, we should consider notating in 12/8 time as an alternative to 4/4, which would expose all the eighth notes without a need for triplet signs. The following example shows these two different notation styles.

TRACK 21

In the first measure of Track 21, each beat is divided in three equal parts. In the second measure, the time signature allows for 12 eighth notes in the measure, but we still subjectively hear four "big beats" at the start of each beamed group of eighth notes. The two measures are therefore functionally equivalent to one another. As a general rule, notate in 4/4 time unless there are a lot of eighth-note triplet signs needed, when it may be less cumbersome to notate in 12/8 time.

Continuing in 4/4 time, we will look at rhythms using 16th notes. In a 16th-note feel, all the "&s" or eighth-note upbeats will fall exactly half-way between the downbeats. However, each eighth-note will now be subdivided differently, when comparing straight-16th and swing-16ths rhythmic feels. In a straight-16th feel, each 16th note is of equal length and divides the eighth note exactly in half (and the beat exactly into quarters):

TRACK 22

Again note the rhythmic counting above the staff. This is how 16th-note rhythms are normally counted. In between the beat numbers (1, 2, 3, 4) and the "&s," we have the "e" on the second 16th note within each beat, and the "a" on the fourth 16th note within each beat.

In a swing-16ths feel, the second and fourth 16th notes in each beat (the "e" and "a" in the rhythmic counting) land two-thirds of the way through each eighth-note, rather than dividing it in half. This is equivalent to playing on the first and third parts of a 16th-note triplet. We still count using "1 e & a," etc., but now each "e" and "a" is played a little later:

TRACK 23

The first measure above looks the same as the previous straight-16ths example, but when a swing-16ths interpretation is applied to it, it sounds equivalent to the second measure above (i.e., the eighth-16th triplets).

Now let's look at various modern pop keyboard parts, for both piano and synthesizers. In each case, we will summarize the rhythms and voicing techniques used. If necessary, please refer back to Chapter 3 to review these techniques as you work through the examples.

The remainder of this chapter is divided into four main sections:

- Piano Comping Techniques

- Piano Arpeggio/Ostinato Techniques

- Synth Comping Techniques

- Synth Arpeggio/Ostinato Techniques

The Comping Techniques sections are based on the various chord voicings developed in Chapter 3, for both piano and synthesizers.

The Arpeggio/Ostinato Techniques sections focus on single-line piano and synth parts, again as developed in Chapter 3.

For most of the music examples in this chapter, there are two audio tracks. The first track is keyboard only (either acoustic piano or synth), with the left-hand part on the left channel, the right-hand part on the right channel, and the hi-hat quarter-note click in the middle. This enables you to practice these examples hands separately, by turning down one channel or the other. (For synth examples with a right-hand part only, this part will be on both the left and right channels).

The second track has a modern pop rhythm section on the left channel and the keyboard part (left and right hands) on the right channel. To play along with the band on these examples, turn down the right channel.

Two of the synth examples in this chapter have three tracks each, instead of two. As well as the play-along track with the rhythm section, we have two separate tracks isolating both the synth bass and the synth comping parts.

# Piano Comping Techniques

We'll start with a straight-eighths piano comping pattern in the style of "Stay With Me" by Sam Smith:

**Piano Comping Technique #1**
**Style of "Stay With Me" by Sam Smith**

TRACK 24
piano only

TRACK 25
piano plus
rhythm section

This example begins with basic triad voicings, with both hands playing the same rhythms. At the end of the odd-numbered measures, the chord voicing lands on the "& of 4," or half-way through beat 4. (See eighth-note counting example in Track 19.) This is an **anticipation** of the following downbeat, i.e., instead of landing on the downbeat, we have landed an eighth-note earlier. This is a garden-variety modern pop rhythmic technique, used to add forward motion to the arrangement.

Beginning in measure 9, the right-hand triads are embellished with arpeggios, filling in the spaces between chords and building the energy level. Toward the end, the C major chord is varied with F/C as a "passing chord;" this implied I–IV–I movement is borrowed from gospel styles and is sometimes referred to as "backcycling."

All of this adds up to a conventional modern pop ballad accompaniment: simple triad voicings and basic eighth-note rhythms with a few anticipations.

Next we move to a straight-16ths piano ballad comping pattern, in the style of "All of Me" by John Legend:

## Piano Comping Technique #2
## Style of "All of Me" by John Legend

TRACK 26
piano only

TRACK 27
piano plus
rhythm section

During measures 1–4 of this example, the right hand is playing dyad voicings (see Tracks 7 and 8), resulting in a lighter texture during this section. Beginning in measure 5, the right hand plays full triads, noticeably increasing the density and energy level. The momentum is further increased in measure 9 with the use of 16th-note arpeggios, mixed in with dyads.

Rhythmically this is a good example of the possibilities available within a 16th-note subdivision. (See Track 22.) Starting in measure 1, the right hand lands on beat 1, then on the last 16th-note of beat 1 (**anticipating** beat 2 by a 16th note), then on the "& of 2" (or half way through beat 2). This rhythm is then repeated during beats 3 and 4 of the measure, and is in keeping with a range of pop and R&B styles.

Beginning in measure 9, the right-hand arpeggios anticipate beats 2 and 4 by 16th notes. This rhythm originates from classic R&B ballad styles, and is easily applicable to modern pop songs.

The left-hand part here is simple, as in many modern pop songs, but still helps to build the energy of the arrangement. In measures 1–8, the left hand plays simple half-note roots, varied with root-5th voicings. Beginning in measure 9, the left hand plays an "alternating octave" pattern using quarter notes, helping to build the energy at this point.

As with all the examples in this book, you are encouraged to apply these patterns to your own songs and progressions. This is the best way to put these stylistic concepts into practice.

Next up we have another straight-16ths piano ballad comping pattern, this time in the style of "Video Games" by Lana Del Rey. Note that the right-hand part is written using bass clef, due to the lower register used.

## Piano Comping Technique #3
## Style of "Video Games" by Lana Del Rey

TRACK 28
piano only

TRACK 29
piano plus
rhythm section

This example has some unusual "chord rhythms" (how frequently the chords change). Most pop ballads change chords either once or twice per measure, but this song often changes chords on every beat, resulting in a more active, unsettled sound.

The piano comping is sparse at the beginning, using quarter-note and half-note rhythms, and employing broad "open triad" voicings. (See Track 9.) Beginning in measure 7, 16th-note subdivisions are added, building the energy from this point. We then return to the sparser rhythms for the final section in measures 11–12.

Apart from the full triads used in measure 10, everywhere else the right hand is playing no more than two notes at once. This lighter "two-part density" is normal in modern pop keyboard parts.

In measures 7–9 and 12, the right-hand two-note voicings get a little more sophisticated: playing the 3rd and 6th of the D6 chord (F♯ and B) in measure 7, the 3rd and 6th of the E6 chord (G♯ and C♯) in measure 8, and the 3rd and 7th of the Dmaj7 chord (F♯ and C♯) in measures 9 and 12. These are customary jazz piano voicings, successfully transplanted here into a modern pop context.

Our next example is a piano comping pattern in the style of "Videotape" by Radiohead. Although the backing track has a straight-16ths subdivision, the piano part sticks to quarter-note rhythms throughout. This type of rhythmic contrast within the song is a feature of certain 21st-century pop styles:

## Piano Comping Technique #4
## Style of "Videotape" by Radiohead

TRACK 30
piano only

TRACK 31
piano plus
rhythm section

This piano part includes a ostinato-type line played by the right hand. In measures 1–5, the right-hand top notes of B♭–A–A–G are repeated over the different changes (Gm, B♭/F, E♭, etc.). A variation of this line (A♭–G–G–F) is then repeated in measures 6–7, and so on. The right hand begins by playing two notes at once (two-part density), increasing to three notes during measures 13–17, helping to build the momentum during this section.

The left-hand part is also building throughout, starting with whole notes in measures 1–9, then moving to an open triad arpeggio in measure 10 (see Track 10), before starting a steady quarter-note pulse along with the right hand from measure 11 onward.

Also note that several chords in this example are placed over their 3rds or 5ths in the bass. (See Track 5.) This enables the left-hand bass line to move in a melodic, step-wise manner, rather than by larger interval skips.

Next up is a more up-tempo, straight-eighths rock piano comping pattern in the style of Adele's "Rolling in the Deep":

## Piano Comping Technique #5
## Style of "Rolling in the Deep" by Adele

TRACK 32
piano only

TRACK 33
piano plus
rhythm section

In the first half of this example, the piano uses sparse dotted-half, quarter, and whole-note rhythms. Starting in measure 9, the right hand plays steady eighth-note triads to drive the groove along. This is a stock technique in both classic and modern pop/rock styles.

In the second half, leading into the even-numbered measures (measures 10, 12, 14, etc.), we are using eighth-note harmonic anticipations: for example, the Bm/D chord is landing on the last eighth note of measure 9 (on the "& of 4"), anticipating the following beat 1. (Review Track 19 as needed, for eighth-note rhythms and counting.) This adds to the forward motion and energy in this section, and regularly occurs in eighth-note pop/rock styles at medium-to-fast tempos.

Although most of the right-hand voicings used here are basic triads and suspensions, there are a few more sophisticated sounds at work in measures 1–8:

- Measure 1: The C6 voicing uses the 6th, 3rd, and 5th (A, E, and G) from bottom to top.

- Measure 3: The G/B voicing uses the root and 5th (G and D) only in the right hand; this creates an open texture over the 3rd in the left hand.

- Measure 4: Adding D to the C major triad creates a C(add9) chord.

- Measure 8: We briefly use a four-part dominant 7th chord (B7) to lead strongly into the following E minor chord.

Next we'll look at a gospel-influenced pop piano comping pattern in the style of "One and Only," also by Adele:

## Piano Comping Technique #6
## Style of "One and Only" by Adele

TRACK 34
piano only

TRACK 35
piano plus
rhythm section

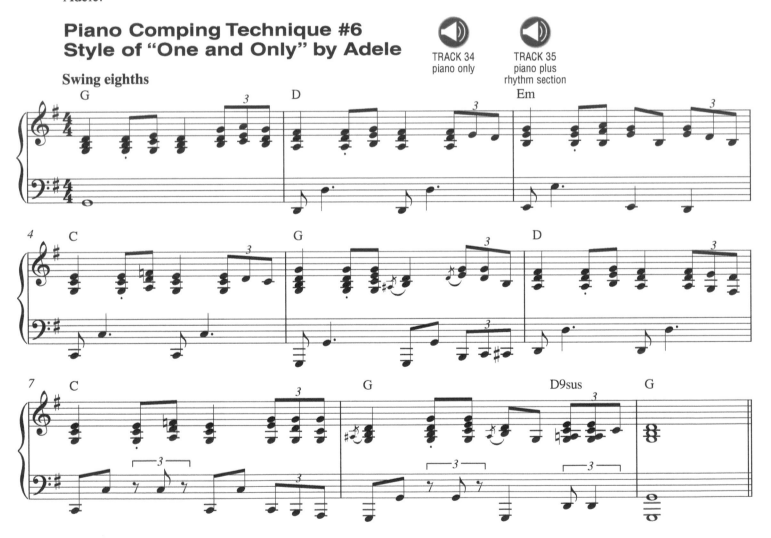

This is a swing-eighths example that also contains eighth-note triplets during beat 4 of each measure except the last. As seen earlier in the text accompanying Track 21, all eighth notes written without triplet signs will be interpreted as swing-eighths. A notation alternative here would be to use 12/8 time; regardless of the time signature, this type of pop/gospel is often described as having a "12/8 feel." Have a listen to the audio track to get familiar with how the eighth-note triplet subdivisions are incorporated into the overall swing-eighths rhythmic feel.

This example uses a several gospel piano devices, including the following:

- Passing triads in the right hand: for example, the C major and A minor triads on the G chord in measure 1, the E minor triad on the D chord in measure 2, etc.

- Bluesy grace notes, including the A♯ to B movement on the G major chord in measures 5 and 8.

- Left-hand "walkup" and "walkdown" movements, at the end of measures 5 and 7.

Have fun with this taste of gospel/pop. For much more information on gospel piano styles, check out my *Pop Piano Book*, published by Hal Leonard Corporation.

Our next example uses interesting syncopations within a straight-16ths rhythmic structure, in the style of "Codex" by Radiohead:

**Piano Comping Technique #7**
**Style of "Codex" by Radiohead**

TRACK 36
piano only

TRACK 37
piano plus
rhythm section

This example has some slightly unconventional chord rhythms, not unusual for Radiohead's style. In the odd-numbered measures, the second chord falls halfway through beat 3 (or on the "& of 3"), rather than directly on beat 3. In the even-numbered measures, the second chord lands on the last 16th note of beat 2, anticipating beat 3 by a 16th note. This all combines to give the example a rather syncopated rhythmic feel.

From a voicing standpoint, we have a representative modern pop mix of triads and suspensions, together with add9 and sus2 chords. (Review these in Chapter 2 as needed.) Starting in measure 9, the left hand picks up more of the syncopations played in the right hand, to help build momentum toward the end of the example.

Next up is a straight-16ths piano ballad comping pattern in the style of "Heart and Soul" by Gary Go:

## Piano Comping Technique #8
## Style of "Heart and Soul" by Gary Go

TRACK 38
piano only

TRACK 39
piano plus
rhythm section

The first four measures of this example are based on half-note triad voicings in the right hand, with a couple of 16th-note partial arpeggio pickups giving forward motion into beat 3 of each measure. Beginning in measure 5, the energy level builds in the right hand with the addition of quarter-note triads.

In measures 5–8 in the right hand, we are adding a "nine-to-one" movement within the second triad in each measure. For example, during beat 4 in measure 5, the E to D movement is a nine-to-one within the D major triad; during beat 4 in measure 6, the A to G movement is a nine-to-one within the G major triad; and so on. This is a good way to add more movement and interest to your pop piano comping parts.

The left hand is playing a sparse and supportive role throughout, sounding the root of the chord on beats 1 and 3 in each measure. Although the right hand is playing 16th-note subdivisions during this example, it sounds straightforward rhythmically as we are not using anticipations (i.e., landing ahead of the beat) as in previous examples.

Now it's time to look at a mid-tempo swing-16ths piano pattern, in the style of "When I Was Your Man" by Bruno Mars:

## Piano Comping Technique #9
## Style of "When I Was Your Man" by Bruno Mars

TRACK 40
piano only

TRACK 41
piano plus
rhythm section

Refer to Track 23 as needed to review the swing-16ths rhythmic feel. Don't forget that, when playing in a swing-16ths style, the downbeats (1, 2, 3, and 4) and the "&s" (the "& of 1," "& of 2," etc.) are still in exactly the same place as for straight 16ths; it's just that the second and fourth 16th notes within the beat are played a little later. Also check out Tracks 40 and 41 to hear how this example sounds.

In measures 1–4, the right-hand part begins with a variation on the alternating eighths device we first heard in Track 6. However, the left hand is adding the all-important 16th-note "thumb pickup" leading into beats 2 and 4 in each measure.

From measure 5 onward, the groove gets busier with the left-hand thumb playing a 16th-note on either side of beat 2, and the right-hand triad anticipating beat 3, and arpeggiating the triad during beat 4. This section is a good template you can apply to many swing-16ths pop and funk progressions.

Continuing with the swing-16ths rhythmic subdivision, next we'll look at a piano pattern in the style of "Bottle It Up" by Sara Bareilles:

## Piano Comping Technique #10
## Style of "Bottle It Up" by Sara Bareilles

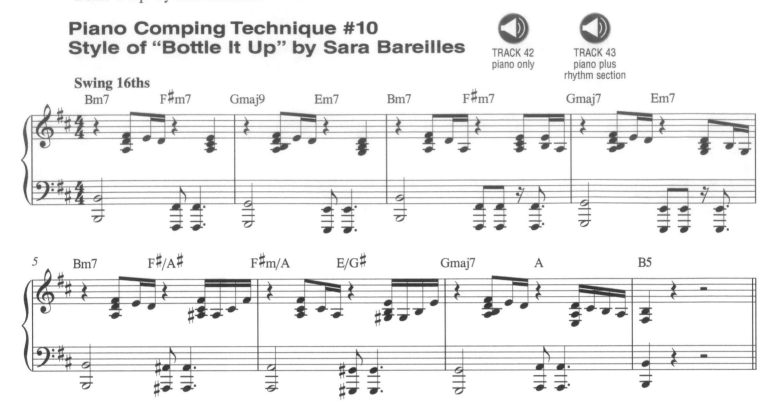

The solid, heavy feel of this example is underpinned by the big left-hand octaves landing on beats 1, 3, and the "& of 3," and the right hand triads landing on beats 2 and 4 (the "backbeats"). At the beginning, the swing-16ths feel is subtle: the last 16th notes of beats 2 and 4 are the only places affected by the swing feel. However, on the rhythm section track, the hi-hat part is playing all the 16th subdivisions, so this may be useful as a reference. The piano part then gets a little busier starting in measure 5, with 16th-note triad arpeggios during beat 4 of each measure.

Note the upper structure triads used to voice some of these chords. (Review Track 13 and accompanying text as needed.) The Bm7, F#m7, and Em7 chords are all voiced by building major triads triads from their 3rds: Bm7 is voiced by playing a D major triad over B in the bass, F#m7 is voiced by playing an A major triad over F# in the bass, and Em7 is voiced by playing a G major triad over E in the bass.

In measure 2, we see a more sophisticated four-part upper structure voicing, where the Gmaj9 chord is voiced by building a four-part Bm7 chord from the 3rd. In measures 5 and 6, some of the chords are placed over their 3rds in the bass, helping to create a melodic left-hand line during this section.

Our final pop piano comping example has a mid-tempo straight-eighths feel, and is in the style of "My Heart Is Open" by Maroon5 and Gwen Stefani:

## Piano Comping Technique #11 — Style of "My Heart Is Open" by Maroon5 and Gwen Stefani

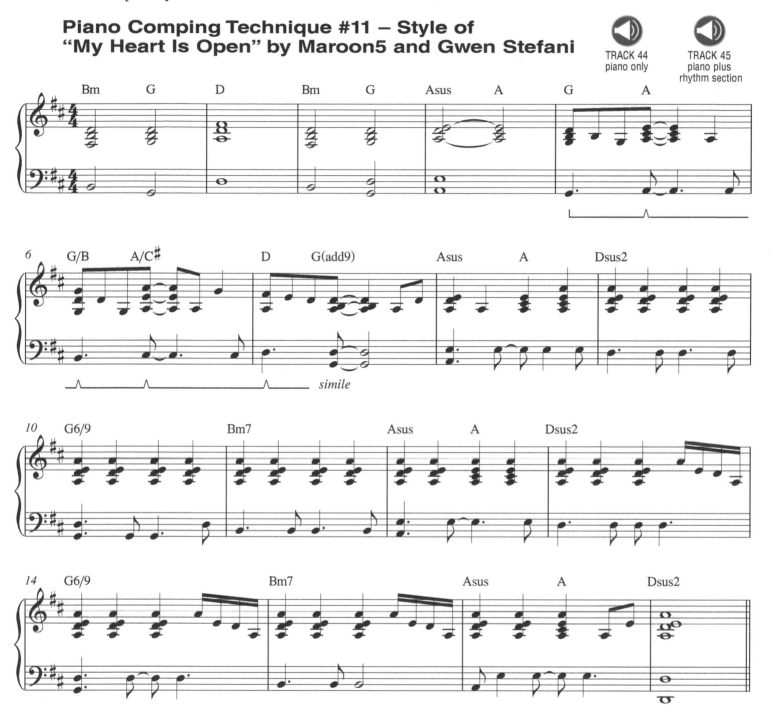

This example uses a modern mix of triad and double-4ths in the right hand. (Review Track 16 and accompanying text as needed, concerning double-4th voicings.) The first eight measures mainly use triad voicings, with some suspensions and add9 chords. Starting in measure 9, the E–A–D double-4th shape is used as the basis of the right-hand voicings: from bottom to top, the first inversion (A–D–E) and second inversion (D–E–A) have been overlapped to create the A–D–E–A four-note voicing used. This is a common and powerful manipulation of the double-4th shape. This shape is then "built from" the 9th of the Dsus2 in measure 9, the 6th of the G6/9 in measure 10, and so on—similar to how the double-4ths were used in Tracks 16 and 17.

Rhythmically, this example also builds in an interesting way. The first four measures begin with basic whole-note and half-note rhythms. Then, starting in measure 5, more eighth-note subdivision is used, leading to an anticipation of beat 3. In measure 9, the right hand plays a steady quarter-note pulse, underpinned by a dotted-quarter/eighth-note repeating pattern in the left hand. In measure 13, the energy builds further with 16th-note arpeggios added during beat 4. This all adds up to a useful modern pop/rock template. As always, you are encouraged to apply this to other songs and progressions of your own.

# Piano Arpeggio/Ostinato Techniques

In the next section of this chapter we'll focus on modern pop piano parts that prominently feature arpeggios or ostinato lines. (Review Tracks 4 and 11–12 as needed.)

We'll start with a straight-eighths piano part in the style of "Demons" by Imagine Dragons:

## Piano Arpeggio/Ostinato Technique #1
## Style of "Demons" by Imagine Dragons

TRACK 46
piano only

TRACK 47
piano plus
rhythm section

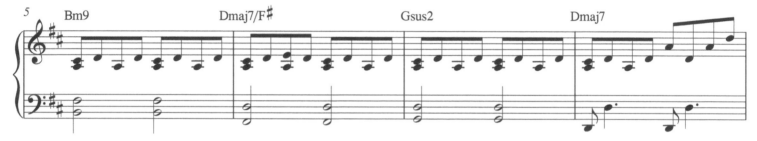

In this example, the ostinato line is the two-measure eighth-note phrase on top of the right-hand part: C♯–D–A–D–C♯–D–A–D in the first measure, and C♯–D–E–D–C♯–D–A–D in the second measure. This is then repeated up until measure 8, then from measure 9 the same line is transposed an octave higher.

This ostinato line is supported at the beginning by solid root-5th voicings in the left hand, and by the single note A landing on downbeats in the right hand. This all creates a sophisticated, yet pop-friendly, sound.

In measure 8, the right hand adds root-and-5th arpeggios on the D major chord, to help change into a higher register as the ostinato line is about to be repeated up an octave. This is supported by busier eighth-note pickups in the left hand.

Starting in measure 9, the higher-register ostinato is supported on beats 1 and 3 by two other chord tones (3rd and 7th on the Bm7, root and 5th on the A major chord, etc.) in the right hand, and by two- or three-note voicings in the left hand (root and 7th on the Bm7, root and 5th on the other chords). Finally, starting in measure 13, the left hand adds open triad arpeggios to further build this section.

Next up is an up-tempo straight-eighths piano ostinato/melody example in the style of "Where the Story Ends" by The Fray:

## Piano Arpeggio/Ostinato Technique #2
## Style of "Where the Story Ends" by The Fray

TRACK 48
piano only

TRACK 49
piano plus
rhythm section

Earlier, I described this example as an "ostinato/melody" because the line varies a little more than an ostinato would. However, the part is still based on a repeating motif or "hook."

The top line (G♯–E–E–F♯–G♯, etc.) is supported mostly by upper structure or partial triads in the right hand. For example, in measure 1 the E major triad is built from the 3rd of the C♯m7 chord; in measure 2, the E major triad is built from the 5th of the A major chord, and so on.

Rhythmic anticipations play a key role in imparting energy to this groove. Throughout measures 2 to 8, both hands land halfway through beat 4 (on the "& of 4"), anticipating beat 1 of the following measure. Starting in measure 9, the left hand plays root-5th patterns or open-triad arpeggios beginning on beat 1, with the right hand anticipating as before.

In measures 14 and 15, the right hand builds further momentum by using octave-doubled triads (triads with the top note doubled one octave lower, creating four notes in total). This is an established device in classic and modern pop piano styles.

When playing this example, make sure you land correctly on all the eighth-note anticipations (i.e., on the "&s"), and use the pedal to achieve a flowing feel throughout.

Now it's time to look at a mid-tempo straight-eighths arpeggio pattern, in the style of "My Heart Is Open" by Maroon5 and Gwen Stefani (based on a different section of the song, as compared to Tracks 44–45):

## Piano Arpeggio/Ostinato Technique #3
## Style of "My Heart Is Open" by Maroon5
## and Gwen Stefani

TRACK 50
piano only

TRACK 51
piano plus
rhythm section

This is probably the most heavily arpeggiated example we've seen so far. In measures 1–8, the right hand is playing arpeggios of the basic chords, supported by root notes in the left hand. The second chord in each measure lands halfway through beat 3 (on the "& of 3"), giving a syncopated feel to this groove.

Starting in measure 9, the energy increases with both hands now playing eighth-note arpeggios: the right hand in a higher register adding octaves and dyads, and the left hand adding the broad sound of open-triad arpeggios.

The busy and rather dense feel of this example won't fit all situations, but in the right song context it might be just what you need. Our final pop piano arpeggio/ostinato example has a straight-16ths ballad feel, and is in the style of "Someone Like You" by Adele:

## Piano Arpeggio/Ostinato Technique #4
## Style of "Someone Like You" by Adele

This example starts with basic half-note triad voicings, with the E major chord placed over its 3rd in the bass in measures 2 and 4. Beginning in measure 5, the right hand plays a continuous 16th-note arpeggio pattern through the changes. This is supported in the left hand by simple root notes and arpeggios in measures 5–8, and by half-note root-5th voicings in measures 9–12. This consistent right-hand arpeggio ballad style is true-to-type for this artist.

When playing this example, ensure you have a legato and flowing style, and use the sustain pedal as indicated.

# Synth Comping Techniques

Now we'll turn our attention to a number of modern pop comping techniques for synths, commencing with a synth comping part in the style of "Good Life" by OneRepublic. Although the backing track has a straight-16ths rhythmic subdivision, the synth part sticks to whole- and half-note rhythms throughout:

**Synth Comping Technique #1**
**Style of "Good Life" by OneRepublic**

 TRACK 54
synth only

 TRACK 55
synth plus
rhythm section

This an example of a "static pad" synth part, as we first heard in Track 14. The synth sound is a mellow analog Oberheim-style synth pad, with a fairly low filter cut-off so that the sound is not too bright. The part starts out with simple half-note and whole-note voicings in the right hand, and any common tones between chords (like the G contained within the C minor and G minor chords in measures 2 and 3) are tied over so that the note is not restruck; this is a common playing technique for this type of smooth, static synth pad.

The voicings used are all basic triads and suspensions, inverted as needed to voice lead from left to right. Starting in measure 9, the left hand plays a simple root-note part to further fill out the sound.

When playing along to the backing tracks for these synth examples, don't worry if you don't have exactly the same sound available as on the recording: any kind of mellow warm pad sound will be fine. And of course you are encouraged to experiment!

Next up are synth parts on an up-tempo straight-eighths example in the style of "Hear Me" by Imagine Dragons:

## Synth Comping Technique #2
## Style of "Hear Me" by Imagine Dragons

TRACK 56
synth only

TRACK 57
synth plus
rhythm section

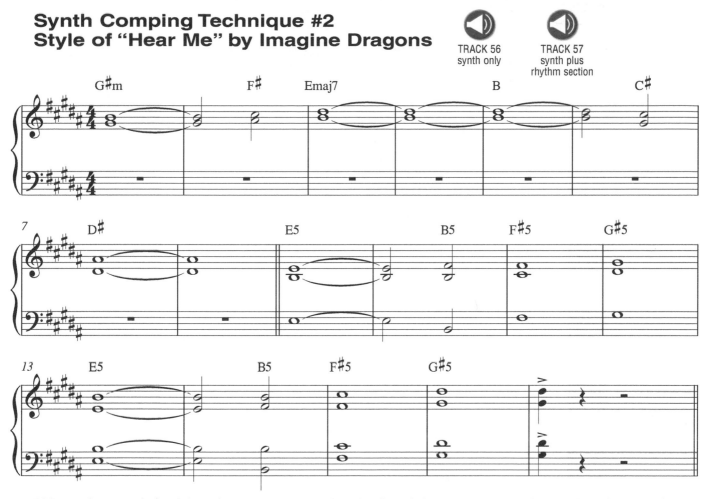

This synth example is divided into two parts. During the first eight measures, an ethereal, breathy synth is playing a series of partial triads and two-note voicings. From measure 9 onward, a big analog synth with "filter swells" (gradually getting brighter as the note is held down) is playing solid root-5th voicings, with the left hand adding root notes.

These synth parts are musically uncomplicated, but can be potent due to the choice of sound and to any motion or changes occurring within the sound—like the filter opening to make the sound brighter.

If you have these two sounds (or similar) on your synthesizer, you can practice the program change needed (at measure 9) to segue from one sound to the other as you play along with the backing track. Well-timed synth program changes are often needed when playing live with a band.

Now let's take a look at some synth bass and comping parts on a mid-tempo straight-16ths example in the style of "Paradise" by Coldplay:

## Synth Comping Technique #3
## Style of "Paradise" by Coldplay

TRACK 58
synth comping and
synth bass only

TRACK 59
Synth comping
plus rhythm
section

TRACK 60
Synth bass plus
rhythm section

In this example, we're going to spotlight both the synth comping and synth bass parts.

- Track 58 has the synth comping on the right channel and the synth bass on the left channel.

- Track 59 has the synth comping on the right channel, and everything else (including the synth bass) on the left channel.

- Track 60 has the synth bass on the right channel, and everything else (including the synth comping) on the left channel.

The sonorities here are orthodox Coldplay: the comping synth is an epic, fat analog sound with octave doubling, and the filter fairly open so that higher frequencies ("buzzyness") can be heard. The bass synth is a big, analog layered sound using sawtooth waves.

The comping synth (shown in the treble clef) uses basic triads and suspensions, with common tones between chords tied over the barline, similar to the synth pads in Tracks 54–55. Rhythmically, beat 3 is being anticipated by an eighth note in each measure.

The bass synth (shown in the bass clef) locks up rhythmically with the comping synth, adding 16th-note connecting tones from beat 2 until the "& of 2" (anticipating beat 3) in each measure.

Next up is a synth part on a slower tempo straight-eighths example in the style of "Retrograde" by James Blake:

## Synth Comping Technique #4
## Style of "Retrograde" by James Blake

TRACK 61
synth only

TRACK 62
synth plus
rhythm section

This right-handed synth part uses dyad voicings for the first eight measures, moving to triads from measure 9 onward. As with previous static synth pad examples, we see common tones tied across the barlines, helping to create a smooth texture.

The sound choice here is interesting for a slow pop ballad: a rather bright and "buzzy" analog synth, with "glide" added. (In a glide, the pitch swoops up to the note played, rather than being on pitch right away.) This choice would be unusual in more classic pop ballad styles; however, these "rules" tend to apply less in today's music.

Note the use of the minor triad placed over its 5th (Gm/D) in measures 3 and 11. This sound is somewhat unusual in modern pop, but is a prominent harmony in the song this example is based on.

On to a more energetic, up-tempo straight-eighths example in the style of "Call Me Maybe" by Carly Rae Jepsen:

## Synth Comping Technique #5
## Style of "Call Me Maybe" by Carly Rae Jepsen

TRACK 63
synth only

TRACK 64
synth plus
rhythm section

The synth used here is a strings sample. When playing along with the backing track, you can use either a synthesized string patch (for example, analog strings) or a strings sample—whatever you have available on your keyboard.

In the first six measures of this example, a continuous eighth-note pulse in the strings drives the groove along. After playing simple root-5th voicings in the first two measures, we then move to inverted double-4ths. (See Track 16.) In measures 3–4 the double-4th G–C–F is in first inversion, and in measures 5–6 the double-4th D–G–C is in second inversion. Both of these double 4ths are built from the 9th of their respective chords (i.e., from the G on the Fsus2, and from the D on the Csus2). Then we return to the simpler root-5th voicings in measures 7–8, this time with the left hand adding root notes in a syncopated pattern.

From measure 9 onward, we're using open triads (see Track 9), with octave doubling added to create four-note voicings. This is an especially strong technique with string sounds, and can help them sound broader and more realistic. Also, the pronounced rhythm pattern at this point creates an identifiable rhythmic hook suitable for modern pop and dance styles.

Now it's time to take a look at a rhythmic synth part on a mid-tempo straight-eighths example in the style of "Fools Gold" by Fitz and the Tantrums:

## Synth Comping Technique #6
## Style of "Fools Gold" by Fitz and the Tantrums

TRACK 65
synth only

TRACK 66
synth plus
rhythm section

This layered synth sound originates from "wavetable" synthesis and has a modern, digital transparency. Play along with a wavetable synth sound if you have one available. Otherwise, any "polysynth" sound with a short attack will do fine.

Here, the right hand is playing a steady eighth-note rhythm, using basic triads and suspensions, and the usual voice leading (using inversions to smoothly connect from one chord to the next). The left hand is following the changes, playing a simple root-note sequence.

The second chord in measures 1–8 anticipates beat 3, landing an eighth note ahead of it, on the "& of 2." As seen earlier, this is a familiar rhythmic figure across the range of pop music styles.

On to a funkier, mid-tempo straight-16ths example in the style of "6AM," again by Fitz and the Tantrums:

## Synth Comping Technique #7
## Style of "6AM" by Fitz and the Tantrums

TRACK 67
synth only

TRACK 68
synth plus
rhythm section

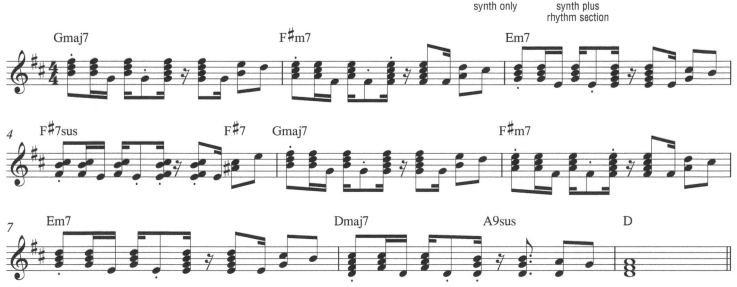

The "synth" used here is actually an organ sample. When playing along with the backing track, you can use either a synthesized organ or an organ sample—whatever you have available on your keyboard.

This example is something of a throwback to old-school R&B/funk styles. The organ part is mostly playing the four-part chords in root position, except for the F#7sus in measure 4. In the first half of each measure, movement is generated by alternating between the upper tones of the chord and the root of the chord, using a syncopated 16th-note pattern typical of funk styles.

In measure 8, the A9sus chord is voiced by building a G major triad from the 7th of the chord, another traditional R&B/pop sound. (Review Track 13 as needed, to see this voicing used on an E9sus chord.)

Our final synth example in this section has an up-tempo straight-16ths feel. It is in the style of "Makes Me Wonder" by Maroon5. Here, we're going to spotlight the synth bass part, which sticks to an eighth-note rhythmic pattern—in contrast to the 16ths used by other instruments on the backing track:

## Synth Comping Technique #8
## Style of "Makes Me Wonder" by Maroon5

TRACK 69
synth only

TRACK 70
synth plus
rhythm section

Just a quick notation point here: when writing bass parts (for example, for electric bass guitar), the convention is to write the part **an octave higher** than where it sounds, as the bass is a transposing instrument. You should also follow this rule when writing synth bass parts. So for example, the first G in Track 69 (written one-and-a-half octaves below middle C) will actually sound one octave lower (two-and-a-half octaves below middle C).

The synth bass sound here is a fat analog sawtooth/square wave layer, ordinary fare in today's pop and dance styles. When playing along, though, feel free to experiment with whatever synth bass sounds you have available.

In measures 1–8, the bass line gets its rhythmic energy by anticipating (landing an eighth note ahead of) beat 3 in each measure, and beat 1 in the even-numbered measures. Also, the line connects between the chord roots by adding notes from the G minor pentatonic scale. (See Chapter 2, page 7.) Beginning in measure 9, the bass line switches to a steady eighth-note pulse playing the roots of the chords, building the energy further at this point.

All of these eighth-note bass rhythms blend nicely with the busier 16th-note guitar and drum parts you can hear on the backing track.

# Synth Arpeggio/Ostinato Techniques

In the final section of this chapter, we'll focus on modern pop synth parts that prominently feature arpeggios or ostinato lines. (Again, review Tracks 4 and 11–12 as needed.)

Our first example is a synth ostinato/melody in the style of "Tiptoe" by Imagine Dragons. Although the backing track has a straight-16ths subdivision, the synth line uses simpler eighth-note rhythms throughout:

### Synth Arpeggio/Ostinato Technique #1
### Style of "Tiptoe" by Imagine Dragons

TRACK 71
synth only

TRACK 72
synth plus
rhythm section

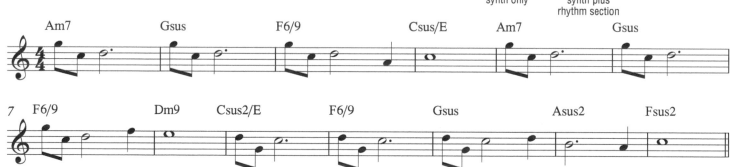

The basis of this ostinato idea is the G–C–D motif used in measures 1–8, inverted to become the D–G–C idea from measure 9 onward. These motifs can also be thought of as arpeggios of inverted double-4th voicings. The ostinato is not strictly repeated throughout, as some melodic variations occur in measures 3–4, 7–8, and 11–13.

The synth sound used here is a Moog-style sawtooth lead synth, which has a classic analog quality suitable for many pop and EDM styles. The relaxed eighth-note rhythms of the synth line are an interesting contrast against the busier 16th-note syncopations of the backing track. Again, these rhythmic contrasts are not unusual in modern pop styles.

Next up is a hybrid arpeggio/ostinato synth part used on an up-tempo straight-eighths example in the style of "Superfuture" by Gary Go:

## Synth Arpeggio/Ostinato Technique #2
## Style of "Superfuture" by Gary Go

TRACK 73
synth only

TRACK 74
synth plus
rhythm section

The synth sound here is a hollow-sounding analog triangle wave, with a short attack and filtered so the sound is not too bright. The rhythms are the same in measures 1–8, and the synth line is created around the tones of each chord.

For example, in measure 1, the line moves between F (the 7th) and G (the root) of the G minor chord; in measure 2, the line moves between D (the 9th) and E♭ (the 3rd) of the C minor chord, and so on.

The line is then varied from measure 9 onward by adding a note on the "& of 3" in each measure, so that the line becomes a continuous series of eighth notes. You are encouraged to experiment by creating this type of line over different chord progressions. This will be useful in your modern pop keyboard arrangements!

Now we'll take a look at a minimalist ostinato synth part used on a swing-eighths example in the style of "Hunger of the Pines" by Alt-J:

## Synth Arpeggio/Ostinato Technique #3
## Style of "Hunger of the Pines" by Alt-J

TRACK 75
synth only

TRACK 76
synth plus
rhythm section

Here, we are using an analog sine and triangle wave layer, with some delay to give space around the sound. The part is simply a series of single notes, placed over the various chords in the example. Normally, this type of part would land on a chord tone (target tone), for each chord in the progression, as follows:

- In measures 1–2, the note A is the root of the A5 (root and 5th only) chord.

- In measures 3–4, the note A is the 3rd of the Fmaj7 chord.

- In measures 5, the note G is the 3rd of the Em7 chord.

- And so on.

When used in the right context, this can add atmosphere and dimension to a song. As always, you are encouraged to experiment with this using different sounds, and over different progressions.

This rather minimal synth part is less common in classic 20th-century pop styles. However, it is in keeping with the "less is more" approach used by certain modern pop artists. For an excellent use of this technique, check out the song this example is based on.

Now it's time to take a look at some synth bass and single-note ostinato/melody parts on an up-tempo straight-eighths example in the style of "If I Had You" by Adam Lambert:

## Synth Arpeggio/Ostinato Technique #4
## Style of "If I Had You" by Adam Lambert

TRACK 77
synth ostinato/
melody and synth
bass only

TRACK 78
synth ostinato/
melody plus
rhythm section

TRACK 79
synth bass plus
rhythm section

In this example, we're going to spotlight both the synth ostinato/melody and synth bass parts.

- Track 77 has the synth bass on the left channel and the synth ostinato/melody on the right channel.

- Track 78 has the synth ostinato/melody on the right channel, and everything else (including the synth bass) on the left channel.

- Track 79 has the synth bass on the right channel, and everything else (including the synth ostinato/melody) on the left channel.

We've used the term "ostinato/melody" again, as the part is based on an ostinato (repeated line), but with some variations as the chords progress.

You often hear these sounds in the music of Adam Lambert and other EDM-influenced pop/dance artists: the ostinato/melody synth is a bright, buzzy trance-like analog sound, and the bass synth is a hard-edged, digital sound that stands out in a mix.

The ostinato/melody synth (shown in the treble clef) enters in the fifth measure and largely copies the rhythm of the synth bass part. The synth line is fashioned around target notes (chord tones) of the various chords: In measure 5, the A is the root of the A minor chord; in measure 6, the C is the 5th of the F major chord; in measure 7, the B is the 3rd of the G major chord, and so on.

The bass synth (shown in the bass clef) is playing the root of each chord on most of the downbeats, with connecting tones and fills toward the end of each measure. All of this adds up to a strong, driving arrangement typical of today's dance/pop styles.

Next up is an ostinato synth part used on an up-tempo straight-eighths example in the style of "If I Lose Myself" by OneRepublic:

## Synth Arpeggio/Ostinato Technique #5
## Style of "If I Lose Myself" by OneRepublic

TRACK 80
synth only

TRACK 81
synth plus
rhythm section

The synth sound here is a "Jupiter-style plucking" analog synth with a short attack. The first ostinato section (measures 1–8) is based around the notes A and C, which are placed over the B♭, Dm, and F chords. A variation occurs in measures 2 and 6, with the notes G and C placed over the C major chords.

The second ostinato section (from measure 9) is based around the notes A and G, placed over the F/A, B♭sus2, and Dm chords. A variation occurs in measure 11, with the notes G and F used over the C5 (root and 5th only) chord, effectively creating a Csus (Csus4) chord at this point.

This type of ostinato is a great way to add momentum to an up-tempo straight-eighths pop groove. Your synth sound should have a short attack (i.e., the sound should speak soon) for this type of part to be effective. Some reverb and/or delay won't hurt either!

Our final synth arpeggio/ostinato example has a mid-tempo straight-16ths feel, and is in the style of "Fireflies" by Owl City:

## Synth Arpeggio/Ostinato Technique #6
## Style of "Fireflies" by Owl City

TRACK 82
synth only

TRACK 83
synth plus
rhythm section

This is a more advanced synth arpeggio example, reflecting the creativity of the song it is based on—one of the best examples of synth-based pop so far in this century.

This example is in the key of D major, and the 16th-note arpeggios are derived from various diatonic chords in the key (A, D, Em, G, etc.). Note the overall range of the arpeggios (greater than one octave) and the rhythmic variations (eighth-notes on beat 3 of the odd-numbered measures, and on beat 1 of the even-numbered measures), all of which combine to create an interesting part.

The synth sound is a hollow triangle wave, with a low-pass filter added to mellow the timbre. This is a great pattern template for you to use over other diatonic triad progressions—and is also good for your technique!

# Chapter 5
# STYLE FILE

In this chapter, we have five examples written in different modern pop keyboard styles. The keyboard parts for these tunes are a mix of chordal comping and arpeggio/ostinato techniques, as developed in Chapter 4. Pieces #1, #2, and #5 are recorded with a grand piano sound, and pieces #3 and #4 are recorded with the synthesizer sounds described in the text.

As we work through these, you'll notice that each is divided into sections, separated by double-barlines. These sections are often four, eight, or sixteen measures in length, and could represent song sections such as Intro, Verse, Chorus, and so on. The great majority of modern pop songs have this kind of structure, and often the keyboard part can be modified or developed as we move from one section of a song to the next.

On the audio tracks, the band (minus the keyboard) is on the left channel, and the keyboard is on the right channel. As well as bass and drums, you'll hear other instruments in the backing band, such as guitar, organ, and additional synth parts. To play along with the band on these tunes, turn down the right channel. "Practice tempo" and "performance tempo" tracks are also provided for each song.

## 1. Too Late

Our first song is a modern rock example in the style of "Apologize" by OneRepublic. This is a straight-eighths groove in the key of D minor, recorded with an acoustic piano sound. The keyboard part is based on the alternating-eighths technique we first heard on Track 6, splitting up the right-hand voicings so that the upper notes land on the downbeats, and the lowest note (played by the thumb) lands on the eighth notes in between.

Note the "half-time feel" comment at the beginning. If you listen to the drum part on the left channel, you'll hear the sidestick played on beat 3 of each measure, instead of on beats 2 and 4 (the normal "backbeats"). This has the effect of making the time seem like it is only "half as fast" as normal 4/4 time. This lends a different intensity to the alternating-eighths keyboard pattern, and is a feature of the song on which this example is based.

The first section (measures 1–16) plays the keyboard pattern through a mix of triads and four-part chords, with added 9ths, and 3rds of the F major chords in the bass. In the second section (measures 17–25), the left hand picks up the pace with half-note octave and root-5th patterns, with the right hand adding syncopation in the even-numbered measures.

By the third section (measures 33–50), the right hand has gained energy by moving up an octave, often playing three notes on the downbeats (instead of two), now supported by open-triad arpeggio patterns in the left hand. Starting in measure 41, the right hand adds octave fills in the odd-numbered measures, further building the energy toward the end.

When practicing this example, make certain you play the alternating-eighths patterns evenly, and use the sustain pedal as indicated. When the right hand starts the octave doubling (measures 41, 43, 45, etc.), be sure to cover the complete octave interval between the thumb and pinky of the right hand, to be in the best position at all times. This may take some practice, but it will be worth it!

TRACK 84
practice
tempo

TRACK 85
performance
tempo

**Half-time feel**

# 2. You Are

Next up is a pop/rock example in the style of "Clocks" by Coldplay. Although this straight-eighths groove is written in the key of F major, it also borrows from the key of F minor, which is why additional flat signs are notated in the music.

This piece is recorded with an acoustic piano sound, and features dense eighth-note arpeggios from beginning to end, like the famous song on which it is based. There is a recurring rhythmic emphasis throughout: In each measure, the descending arpeggio patterns start on beat 1, then halfway through beat 2 (the "& of 2"), then on beat 4. This rhythm is also accented in the backing track, and is a conventional modern and alternative rock rhythmic figure.

The first section (measures 1–16) splits into two parts: In measures 1–8 the right hand establishes the basic arpeggio figure, when is then doubled an octave lower in the left hand in measures 9–16. In the second section (measures 17–32), each hand begins to arpeggiate a different inversion of the same triad and suspension. For example, in measure 18, the A♭ major triads are played in first inversion in the right hand, and in root position in the left hand. This is a useful way to broaden the sound at this point.

In the third section (measures 33–41), we have a combination of an ostinato-based part in the right hand together with arpeggios in the left hand. In measure 33, we see that the Bb–A–F line is repeated over the chords in that section, substituting the E♭ for the F over the Cm7 chord. This adds interesting chord extensions and creates a more sophisticated and dense sound overall. Meanwhile, the left hand is repeating the basic chord arpeggios played earlier.

When practicing this tune, use the sustain pedal as indicated, and feel free to emphasize the rhythmic accents (beat 1, the "& of 2," and beat 4) in each measure, as mentioned above. Have fun!

52

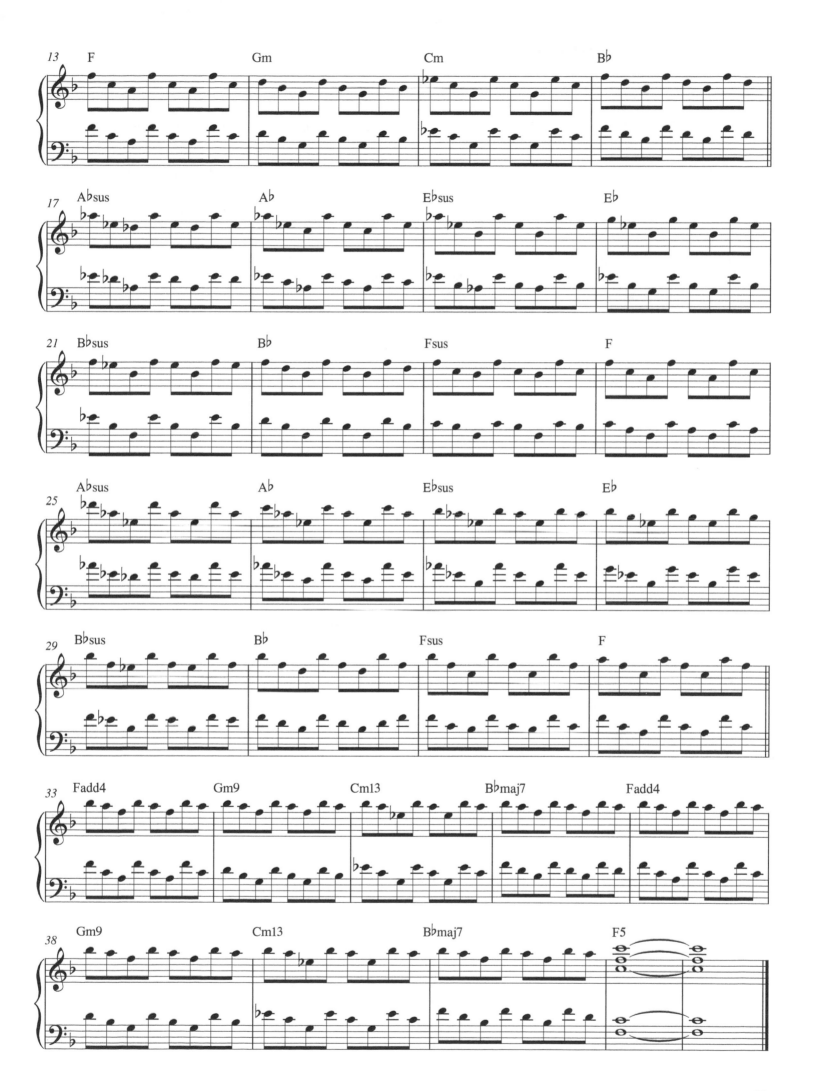

# 3. Don't You Forget

Our next piece is a modern pop synth part in the style of "It's My Life" by No Doubt. This is a mid-tempo straight-eighths groove in the key of D major, although the Verse sections borrow from other keys. The synth sound is a fat analog polysynth with the filter fairly open, allowing the higher harmonics to come through.

The first section (measures 1–16) splits into two parts: In measures 1–8, the right-hand synth part plays static pads with basic triads and suspensions. Here, rhythmic interest is generated by anticipating beat 1 (i.e., landing on the previous "& of 4" and tying across the barline) of the even-numbered measures. In measures 9–16, the left hand joins in, playing solid root-5th voicings on each chord.

In the second section (measures 17–24), the chord rhythms and anticipations get busier, with both hands playing mostly at the same time. Here, the right hand is playing basic or upper structure triads, while the left hand adds root notes or occasional root-7th intervals.

The third section (measures 25–32) repeats the chord progression from the first section, now with more rhythmic pads and anticipations. This leads to the fourth section (measures 33–40), which repeats the second section structure, now adding more arpeggios in the right hand. Finally, the last section (measures 41–49) is a Coda that breaks out into a continuous right-hand arpeggio pattern over the D major and A minor chords.

When practicing this example, try to play the synth part as smooth and legato as you can, except for the third section (measures 25–32) where you should accent the rhythms and observe the rests.

TRACK 88
practice
tempo

TRACK 89
performance
tempo

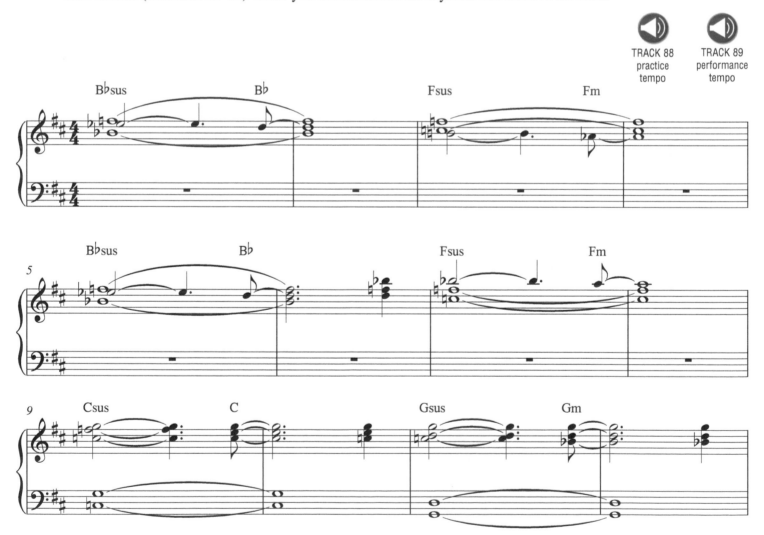

# 4. Happy Technology

Let's take a look at a modern synth-pop example in the style of "The Veldt" by Deadmau5 and Chris Jones. This is an up-tempo piece in the key of E minor, and features a pulsating eighth-note polysynth part throughout, typical of EDM-influenced pop styles.

This example is different from the other Style File pieces, in that what we see on the printed music does not correspond to the eighth-note pulses we hear on the recording. This is because the pulsating synth part is generated from an LFO (low-frequency oscillator) being used to modify the filter (i.e., to open and close it over time). This gives the effect of re-starting the chord on every eighth-note, while the voicing is being held down on the keyboard. (This type of tempo-synced synth part is common in today's pop and EDM styles.) In other words, the written music reflects what is physically being played, but the tempo-sync is transforming that into eighth-note pulses.

If you have tempo-sync capabilities on your synth, program it to start on every eighth note. If playing along with the practice track, set the tempo to 88bpm; if playing along with the performance track, set the tempo to 128bpm. If you then play the part as written, the eighth-note pulses will be generated. Otherwise, you can simply play the part as written, without tempo-sync; this will result in more of a "static pad" that nevertheless will work with the track. You can also try to play the eighth notes manually, extrapolating from the written part.

The first section (measures 1–24) starts out within different suspensions on an E minor chord, before settling into the main sequence starting in measure 9. In the second section (bridge) beginning in measure 25, we momentarily move to the key of C major with a more active top-line melody. Starting in measure 37, the main sequence returns, followed by a repeat of the suspended E minor chords to finish off the example. The voicings used are a combination of basic triads, suspensions, and add9 chords.

If you are using tempo-sync on your synth, try to play the written rhythms as precisely as you can, so that the voicings sync up correctly with the backing track. As mentioned above, you can still play along, even if you don't use tempo-sync. It'll just sound a little different.

TRACK 90
practice
tempo

TRACK 91
performance
tempo

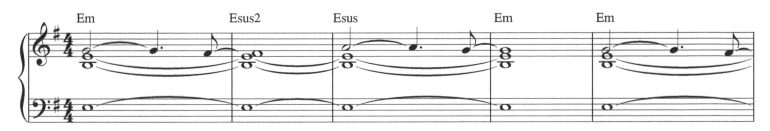

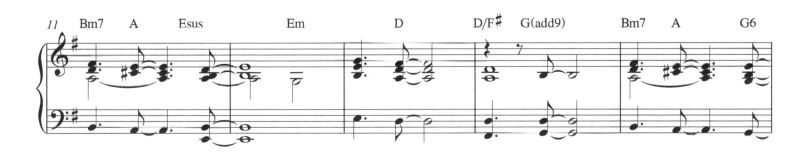

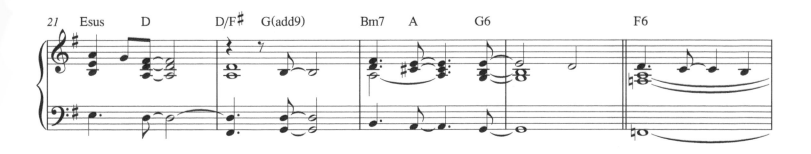

# 5. Everyone Ends Up Alone

Our last tune in this section is an up-tempo pop/rock example in the style of "You Found Me" by The Fray. This piece is in the key of C major and is built around a piano ostinato that is stock-in-trade for this band's writing and arranging.

Harmonically, the main ostinato figure uses the tonic and 5th degrees of the key (C and G), which are good notes to place over other chords from the same key, as we see here. An interesting rhythmic effect is created by the ostinato landing on all the eighth-note subdivisions except for beats 1 or 3 (the so-called "primary beats") in most measures: This results in a continuous series of anticipations that propels the groove along.

The first section (measures 1–16) introduces this right-hand ostinato figure, over mostly whole-note voicings in the left hand. The energy begins to build from measure 9 onward, with dyads added on upbeats in the right hand, and a half-note pattern beginning in the left hand.

In the second section (measures 17–32), the right hand switches to a more melodic part, with octave doubling and eighth-note fills, while the left hand adds open triads and anticipations.

In the third section (measures 33–40), the right-hand ostinato figure returns one octave higher than before, over a busier chord rhythm (now two chords per measure). This leads into the fourth section (measures 41–48), which reprises the right-hand melody from the second section, an octave higher. The left hand now has room to add supporting voicings, triads and suspensions, around the middle C area. Finally, in measures 49–56, the primary right-hand ostinato returns over the busier chord rhythm, leading into a melodic ending for the last four measures.

When playing this piece, use the sustain pedal as indicated to ensure that the right-hand ostinato figures flow correctly across the changes. Also, make sure both hands lock up correctly with the anticipated rhythms in measures 41–48. Have fun!

TRACK 92
practice
tempo

TRACK 93
performance
tempo

# KEYBOARD STYLE SERIES

## THE COMPLETE GUIDE!

*These book/audio packs provide focused lessons that contain valuable how-to insight, essential playing tips, and beneficial information for all players. From comping to soloing, comprehensive treatment is given to each subject. The companion audio features many of the examples in the book performed either solo or with a full band.*

### BEBOP JAZZ PIANO
*by John Valerio*

This book provides detailed information for bebop and jazz keyboardists on: chords and voicings, harmony and chord progressions, scales and tonality, common melodic figures and patterns, comping, characteristic tunes, the styles of Bud Powell and Thelonious Monk, and more.

00290535 Book/Online Audio ..............................$21.99

### BEGINNING ROCK KEYBOARD
*by Mark Harrison*

This comprehensive book/audio package will teach you the basic skills needed to play beginning rock keyboard. From comping to soloing, you'll learn the theory, the tools, and the techniques used by the pros. The accompanying audio demonstrates most of the music examples in the book.

00311922 Book/Online Audio ..............................$16.99

### BLUES PIANO
*by Mark Harrison*

With this book/audio pack, you'll learn the theory, the tools, and even the tricks that the pros use to play the blues. Covers: scales and chords; left-hand patterns; walking bass; endings and turnarounds; right-hand techniques; how to solo with blues scales; crossover licks; and more.

00311007 Book/Online Audio ..............................$22.99

### BOOGIE-WOOGIE PIANO
*by Todd Lowry*

From learning the basic chord progressions to inventing your own melodic riffs, you'll learn the theory, tools and techniques used by the genre's best practicioners.

00117067 Book/Online Audio ..............................$17.99

### BRAZILIAN PIANO
*by Robert Willey and Alfredo Cardim*

*Brazilian Piano* teaches elements of some of the most appealing Brazilian musical styles: choro, samba, and bossa nova. It starts with rhythmic training to develop the fundamental groove of Brazilian music.

00311469 Book/Online Audio ..............................$19.99

### CONTEMPORARY JAZZ PIANO
*by Mark Harrison*

From comping to soloing, you'll learn the theory, the tools, and the techniques used by the pros. The full band tracks on the audio feature the rhythm section on the left channel and the piano on the right channel, so that you can play along with the band.

00311848 Book/Online Audio ..............................$19.99

### COUNTRY PIANO
*by Mark Harrison*

Learn the theory, the tools, and the tricks used by the pros to get that authentic country sound. This book/audio pack covers: scales and chords, walkup and walkdown patterns, comping in traditional and modern country, Nashville "fretted piano" techniques and more.

00311052 Book/Online Audio ..............................$19.99

### GOSPEL PIANO
*by Kurt Cowling*

Discover the tools you need to play in a variety of authentic gospel styles, through a study of rhythmic devices, grooves, melodic and harmonic techniques, and formal design. The accompanying audio features over 90 tracks, including piano examples as well as the full gospel band.

00311327 Book/Online Adio ..............................$19.99

### INTRO TO JAZZ PIANO
*by Mark Harrison*

From comping to soloing, you'll learn the theory, the tools, and the techniques used by the pros. The accompanying audio demonstrates most of the music examples in the book. The full band tracks feature the rhythm section on the left channel and the piano on the right channel, so that you can play along with the band.

00312088 Book/Online Audio ..............................$19.99

### JAZZ-BLUES PIANO
*by Mark Harrison*

This comprehensive book will teach you the basic skills needed to play jazz-blues piano. Topics covered include: scales and chords • harmony and voicings • progressions and comping • melodies and soloing • characteristic stylings.

00311243 Book/Online Audio ..............................$19.99

### JAZZ-ROCK KEYBOARD
*by T. Lavitz*

Learn what goes into mixing the power and drive of rock music with the artistic elements of jazz improvisation in this comprehensive book and CD package. This instructional tool delves into scales and modes, and how they can be used with various chord progressions to develop the best in soloing chops.

00290536 Book/CD Pack..............................$17.95

### LATIN JAZZ PIANO
*by John Valerio*

This book is divided into three sections. The first covers Afro-Cuban (Afro-Caribbean) jazz, the second section deals with Brazilian influenced jazz – Bossa Nova and Samba, and the third contains lead sheets of the tunes and instructions for the play-along audio.

00311345 Book/Online Audio ..............................$19.99

### MODERN POP KEYBOARD
*by Mark Harrison*

From chordal comping to arpeggios and ostinatos, from grand piano to synth pads, you'll learn the theory, the tools, and the techniques used by the pros. The online audio demonstrates most of the music examples in the book.

00146596 Book/Online Audio ..............................$19.99

### NEW AGE PIANO
*by Todd Lowry*

From melodic development to chord progressions to left-hand accompaniment patterns, you'll learn the theory, the tools and the techniques used by the pros. The accompanying 96-track CD demonstrates most of the music examples in the book.

00117322 Book/CD Pack..............................$16.99

### POST-BOP JAZZ PIANO
*by John Valerio*

This book/audio pack will teach you the basic skills needed to play post-bop jazz piano. Learn the theory, the tools, and the tricks used by the pros to play in the style of Bill Evans, Thelonious Monk, Herbie Hancock, McCoy Tyner, Chick Corea and others. Topics covered include: chord voicings, scales and tonality, modality, and more.

00311005 Book/Online Audio ..............................$19.99

### PROGRESSIVE ROCK KEYBOARD
*by Dan Maske*

You'll learn how soloing techniques, form, rhythmic and metrical devices, harmony, and counterpoint all come together to make this style of rock the unique and exciting genre it is.

00311307 Book/Online Audio ..............................$19.99

### R&B KEYBOARD
*by Mark Harrison*

From soul to funk to disco to pop, you'll learn the theory, the tools, and the tricks used by the pros with this book/audio pack. Topics covered include: scales and chords, harmony and voicings, progressions and comping, rhythmic concepts, characteristic stylings, the development of R&B, and more! Includes seven songs.

00310881 Book/Online Audio ..............................$22.99

### ROCK KEYBOARD
*by Scott Miller*

Learn to comp or solo in any of your favorite rock styles. Listen to the audio to hear your parts fit in with the total groove of the band. Includes 99 tracks! Covers: classic rock, pop/rock, blues rock, Southern rock, hard rock, progressive rock, alternative rock and heavy metal.

00310823 Book/Online Audio ..............................$17.99

### ROCK 'N' ROLL PIANO
*by Andy Vinter*

Take your place alongside Fats Domino, Jerry Lee Lewis, Little Richard, and other legendary players of the '50s and '60s! This book/audio pack covers: left-hand patterns; basic rock 'n' roll progressions; right-hand techniques; straight eighths vs. swing eighths; glisses; crushed notes, rolls, note clusters and more. Includes six complete tunes.

00310912 Book/Online Audio ..............................$19.99

### SALSA PIANO
*by Hector Martignon*

From traditional Cuban music to the more modern Puerto Rican and New York styles, you'll learn the all-important rhythmic patterns of salsa and how to apply them to the piano. The book provides historical, geographical and cultural background info, and the 50+-tracks includes piano examples and a full salsa band percussion section.

00311049 Book/Online Audio ..............................$19.99

### SMOOTH JAZZ PIANO
*by Mark Harrison*

Learn the skills you need to play smooth jazz piano – the theory, the tools, and the tricks used by the pros. Topics covered include: scales and chords; harmony and voicings; progressions and comping; rhythmic concepts; melodies and soloing; characteristic stylings; discussions on jazz evolution.

00311095 Book/Online Audio ..............................$19.99

### STRIDE & SWING PIANO
*by John Valerio*

Learn the styles of the stride and swing piano masters, such as Scott Joplin, Jimmy Yancey, Pete Johnson, Jelly Roll Morton, James P. Johnson, Fats Waller, Teddy Wilson, and Art Tatum. This book/audio pack covers classic ragtime, early blues and boogie woogie, New Orleans jazz and more. Includes 14 songs.

00310882 Book/Online Audio ..............................$22.99

### WORSHIP PIANO
*by Bob Kauflin*

From chord inversions to color tones, from rhythmic patterns to the Nashville Numbering System, you'll learn the tools and techniques needed to play piano or keyboard in a modern worship setting.

00311425 Book/Online Audio ..............................$19.99

## HAL•LEONARD®

Prices, contents, and availability
subject to change without notice.

**www.halleonard.com**

0722
167

# PLAY PIANO LIKE A PRO!

## AMAZING PHRASING – KEYBOARD
### 50 Ways to Improve Your Improvisational Skills
*by Debbie Denke*

*Amazing Phrasing* is for any keyboard player interested in learning how to improvise and how to improve their creative phrasing. This method is divided into three parts: melody, harmony, and rhythm & style. The online audio contains 44 full-band demos for listening, as well as many play-along examples so you can practice improvising over various musical styles and progressions.

00842030 Book/Online Audio............................... $16.99

## BEBOP LICKS FOR PIANO
### A Dictionary of Melodic Ideas for Improvisation
*by Les Wise*

Written for the musician who is interested in acquiring a firm foundation for playing jazz, this unique book/audio pack presents over 800 licks. By building up a vocabulary of these licks, players can connect them together in endless possibilities to form larger phrases and complete solos. The book includes piano notation, and the online audio contains helpful note-for-note demos of every lick.

00311854 Book/Online Audio............................... $17.99

## BOOGIE WOOGIE FOR BEGINNERS
*by Frank Paparelli*

A short easy method for learning to play boogie woogie, designed for the beginner and average pianist. Includes: exercises for developing left-hand bass • 25 popular boogie woogie bass patterns • arrangements of "Down the Road a Piece" and "Answer to the Prayer" by well-known pianists • a glossary of musical terms for dynamics, tempo and style.

00120517 ............................................... $10.99

## HAL LEONARD JAZZ PIANO METHOD
*by Mark Davis*

This is a comprehensive and easy-to-use guide designed for anyone interested in playing jazz piano – from the complete novice just learning the basics to the more advanced player who wishes to enhance their keyboard vocabulary. The accompanying audio includes demonstrations of all the examples in the book! Topics include essential theory, chords and voicings, improvisation ideas, structure and forms, scales and modes, rhythm basics, interpreting a lead sheet, playing solos, and much more!

00131102 Book/Online Audio............................... $19.99

## INTROS, ENDINGS & TURNAROUNDS FOR KEYBOARD
### Essential Phrases for Swing, Latin, Jazz Waltz, and Blues Styles
*by John Valerio*

Learn the intros, endings and turnarounds that all of the pros know and use! This new keyboard instruction book by John Valerio covers swing styles, ballads, Latin tunes, jazz waltzes, blues, major and minor keys, vamps and pedal tones, and more.

00290525 ............................................... $12.99

## JAZZ PIANO TECHNIQUE
### Exercises, Etudes & Ideas for Building Chops
*by John Valerio*

This one-of-a-kind book applies traditional technique exercises to specific jazz piano needs. Topics include: scales (major, minor, chromatic, pentatonic, etc.), arpeggios (triads, seventh chords, upper structures), finger independence exercises (static position, held notes, Hanon exercises), parallel interval scales and exercises (thirds, fourths, tritones, fifths, sixths, octaves), and more! The online audio includes 45 recorded examples.

00312059 Book/Online Audio............................... $19.99

## JAZZ PIANO VOICINGS
### An Essential Resource for Aspiring Jazz Musicians
*by Rob Mullins*

The jazz idiom can often appear mysterious and difficult for musicians who were trained to play other types of music. Long-time performer and educator Rob Mullins helps players enter the jazz world by providing voicings that will help the player develop skills in the jazz genre and start sounding professional right away – without years of study! Includes a "Numeric Voicing Chart," chord indexes in all 12 keys, info about what range of the instrument you can play chords in, and a beginning approach to bass lines.

00310914 ............................................... $19.99

## OSCAR PETERSON – JAZZ EXERCISES, MINUETS, ETUDES & PIECES FOR PIANO

Legendary jazz pianist Oscar Peterson has long been devoted to the education of piano students. In this book he offers dozens of pieces designed to empower the student, whether novice or classically trained, with the technique needed to become an accomplished jazz pianist.

00311225 ............................................... $14.99

## PIANO AEROBICS
*by Wayne Hawkins*

*Piano Aerobics* is a set of exercises that introduces students to many popular styles of music, including jazz, salsa, swing, rock, blues, new age, gospel, stride, and bossa nova. In addition, there is a online audio with accompaniment tracks featuring professional musicians playing in those styles.

00311863 Book/Online Audio ..................... $19.99

## PIANO FITNESS
### A Complete Workout
*by Mark Harrison*

This book will give you a thorough technical workout, while having fun at the same time! The accompanying online audio allows you to play along with a rhythm section as you practice your scales, arpeggios, and chords in all keys. Instead of avoiding technique exercises because they seem too tedious or difficult, you'll look forward to playing them. Various voicings and rhythmic settings, which are extremely useful in a variety of pop and jazz styles, are also introduced.

00311995 Book/Online Audio............................... $19.99

**HAL•LEONARD®**
7777 W. BLUEMOUND RD. P.O. BOX 13819
MILWAUKEE, WISCONSIN 53213
www.halleonard.com

*Prices, contents, and availability subject to change without notice.*